FOUR MAKERS OF THE
AMERICAN MIND

FOUR MAKERS OF THE AMERICAN MIND: EMERSON, THOREAU, WHITMAN, AND MELVILLE

A Bicentennial Tribute

New Essays by ROBERT E. SPILLER,
J. LYNDON SHANLEY, FLOYD STOVALL,
and LEON HOWARD

Edited and with a Preface by
THOMAS EDWARD CRAWLEY

DURHAM, N.C.
DUKE UNIVERSITY PRESS
1976

© 1976, Duke University Press

L.C.C. card no. 76–24188

I.S.B.N. 0–8223–0372–8

Printed in the United States of
America by Heritage Printers, Inc.

Contents

Preface

Hampden-Sydney College was founded in 1776; it is the nation's bicentennial college and has been officially designated such by the American Revolution Bicentennial Administration. The significance of its role as an institution of the Revolution is suggested by the fact that both Patrick Henry and James Madison served on its first board of trustees. One stated purpose of the founders was "to form good men and good citizens in an atmosphere of sound learning."

As a part of a four-year bicentennial celebration the college designated the academic year 1974–1975 for an exploration of "America's Cultural Heritage." In the area of literature the general topic selected was "The American Character as Reflected and/or Projected in the Writings of Emerson, Thoreau, Whitman, and Melville." The college sought out four of the nation's most distinguished scholars—Leon Howard, J. Lyndon Shanley, Robert E. Spiller, and Floyd Stovall—and brought them to its campus in April of 1975 to participate in a symposium capping, so to speak, the literary activities of the year. Each scholar was left completely free to relate his particular author to the general theme in any way he might find appropriate. The result was the variety of approaches to be found in the essays comprising the body of this book. Each essay is a highly original "backward glance" by an eminent authority; taken together they are the fruits of lifetime studies of four major American authors by four major American scholars.

The purpose of this year of exploration was to arrive at a reasonably comprehensive view of what these key mid-nineteenth century literary figures did consciously through their writings in giving voice to or projecting the American character as a shaping influence through which the values of the American experiment, as they saw them, might be clarified, strengthened, and ultimately realized. This involved such basic undertakings as the encouragement of the establishment, on a new continent, of an original relationship with nature; the clarification and expansion of philosophical, and even religious, foundations for democracy; the thoughtful consideration of the relationships and obligations of this democracy to the past; the imaginative creation of the great composite democratic individual, the complete citizen of this new democracy; or the adumbration of the grand role of the new individual and the new society in human history. Emerson, Thoreau, and Whitman, each in his own way, felt obligated to serve some such ends. And Melville should also be included. In him, despite his dark vision, we see surprising manifestations of the bright hopes of his age for the future of this country. A basic thesis is that these writers came into their own at just the right moment in our history to accept with confidence and to expound with vigor the essence of the American dream. This could not have been done as effectively at any earlier or later date.

As we look back, Emerson, Thoreau, Whitman, and Melville seem auspiciously poised in time for fulfilling the peculiar challenge which they felt to be their own as American writers. That challenge, or those challenges, can be described in many different ways. F. O. Matthiessen identifies as the common denominator of these strikingly different writers their devotion to the possibilities of democracy and to the full exploration and delineation of those possibilities in their works. He describes them as "the builders of the myth of the common man," of man "in his full revolutionary and democratic splendor as the base and measure of society." The type of this common man, Matthiessen suggests, is Christ, in his "union of suffering and majesty." Thus, Matthiessen recalls for us Whitman's use of the Christ-figure as the hero of *Leaves of Grass* and the conviction of all of these men that all valid democratic ideals were simply political manifestations of the American commitment to Christianity. Melville, for instance, speaks of his worthy American colleagues as writers "who breathe that unshackled, democratic spirit of Christianity in all things, which now takes the practical lead in this world, though at the same time led by ourselves—us Americans." All four of our writers were vitally interested in creating a literature of great aesthetic value which at the same time would be proper to the United States of America as a growing and potentially perfect democracy.

Their dreams, for both their country and their art, were based on the belief that America was to be the culmination of ages of human yearning for freedom, brotherhood, and unity. Whitman, in particular, saw in the development of this nation, in the spanning of the American continent, the great symbol of a newly emerging unity. The globe was being finally rounded; through the American experience East and West, Asia and Europe, would meet and be reconciled. For him the East always stood for unity and spirituality; the West, for variety and materiality. Here were thesis and antithesis; American democracy by assuring at once individuality, equality, and brotherhood would achieve the meaningful synthesis. Here is what our mid-century idealists felt to be our "manifest destiny." It was not original with them, to be sure, but they gave it a new poetic expression. For these men, to give poetic expression to anything was to evaluate and judge, lovingly and finally. It is this role of evaluator and judge that Emerson has in mind when he declares that "the birth of a poet is the principal event in chronology." Or again, here are Whitman's "native voices," shaping voices, and whether or not they appear to be altogether valid is not the point. They are expressing ideals, and sometimes genuine fears, without some knowledge of which a man cannot understand fully how we have arrived where we are as a nation. The loss or compromise of a dream or point of view does not necessarily annul its value or usefulness in understanding developments in which it played a shaping role.

It just may be that the time is ripe for a re-evaluation of such aspects of mid-nineteenth century idealism and its literary expression for far more significant reasons than the simple fact that we are celebrating our bicentennial. As the result of two World Wars at least two generations of Americans have shared a deep-seated distrust of strong national feeling. In 1955 Milton Hindus was being rather daring when he wrote, "the very qualities of Whitman which once made me suspicious of his motivations in the days when Hitler and Mussolini gave a bad name to every legitimate national aspiration have become increasingly the most important in my mind." And Shapiro, for example, laments the fact that the twentieth-century poet avoids the commitment "to adumbrate the meaning of America." There may be a generation of young poets upon us who will, in a new way, find their "usable past" in aspects of the dynamic art, if not always the positive faith, of our mid-nineteenth century literary idealists.

The appropriateness of such a theme for a bicentennial celebration is quite obvious; but more important, these writers were committed patriots in such a way that the shape of their art and its distinctive aesthetic values cannot be understood without taking into account that commitment. We are involved in an attempt to understand aspects of both the American character and the art of four of our greatest writers. As an immediate orientation for the essays that follow, it may be well to consider briefly a few instances of the ways in which the Americanism and the art of these writers tend to fuse.

Each of these writers in his own way came to feel that the first step toward a great native literature of our own involved the assimilation of vast amounts of American materials; and each began that brave process in the faith that, having assimilated them, the appropriate literary forms, in time, would come. And they did. Each gave himself to his country and was not betrayed. The giving was the secret of the gaining. One is reminded of William Carlos Williams' comment on the thinness of most of our Puritan art: "The Puritan remained European, fearful of emotional contact with a new Eden-like land. Instead of embracing it, he exploited it." Emerson, Thoreau, Whitman, and Melville, each in his own way, were embracers, not so much as great patriots, though they were that, but as awakened and inspired poetic spirits. Theirs was the giant step toward a genuinely great and genuinely American culture; their literary achievements make it abundantly clear that the American longing for a great literature rooted in our particular time and place was anything but a matter of mere pride or shallow patriotism, that it was a valid aesthetic longing.

It is a commonplace to see Emerson's Americanism in terms of a paradoxical idealism and practicality. But Emerson himself seems not to have felt any such sharp dichotomy. "In all my lectures," he declares, "I have taught one doctrine, namely, the infinitude of the private man." Note the key words: infinitude, private. Such a statement is the point from which any consideration of Emerson as an artist and thinker must start. He did not want his idealism divorced from the material facts of his age.

Together they provide the full dimension of his vision. It seemed to Emerson that he should, and could, write both about Universal Man and about man as a democratic citizen. He had no intention of attempting less, and it seems to me, he did so with consummate skill. Had not his own growth been fostered not only by the renascence of idealistic philosophy, but also by his eager apprehension of the possibilities of a practical American democracy? His belief in the infinitude of the private man was a democratic doctrine. On it was grounded his beliefs in the supreme worth of the individual and of the equality of all men. And he felt it a part of his calling to explain each individual man to himself. Such an explanation, as he conceived it, demanded both moral philosophy and the most exacting scrutiny of his own immediate American experience. He was given to untrammeled philosophical speculation, but he was also possessed of a strong Yankee practicality. He gave free rein to both.

Indeed, it was his sense of calling to high thinking and a practical American application of it that led him to the lecture platform. Even as a boy he had recognized oratory as the one branch of literature in which America had formed a living tradition of her own. With the Revolution it had spread from the pulpit to the political forum, and he declared that it was eminently the one art that should flourish in a democracy, since it calls out the highest resources of character among the people. But even more important, from the point of view of his literary career, his lecturing was destined to give to his mature art its unique form and content and purpose, rendering him the epitome of the American style. For by his middle thirties he had settled down to the realization that the lecture, drawn from the daily harvest of his journals, and finally distilled into an essay, was to be peculiarly his art form, his literary genre.

I am convinced that another thing that has given his art its unique qualities is his tendency always to see himself in the role of teacher, and in that sense inspirer and instigator. He said of himself, and meant it, that his greatest joy was that of seeing his own accomplishments surpassed by those of his pupils. This also accounts for the frequently encountered observation that though he is one of our greatest writers, he produced no literary masterpiece. If he is truly the teacher, then his work must be open-ended, primarily a point of departure only. That, indeed, Thoreau and Whitman and Melville found it to be. Each in his own way respected Emerson and was moved by his thought and expression; but Thoreau objected from time to time, Whitman objected often, and Melville openly rebelled. Be that as it may, they were all nourished spiritually, and Melville in particular grew artistically richer because of his need to devastate Mr. Emerson. Emerson was, in short, the intellectual catalyst of his time. As such, he never sought assent; rather, to use his own well-chosen word, he sought *vent*. The only proper time for reading another's book, he insisted, is when one is unable to write his own. Even when he is obviously inviting an intellectual confrontation, one senses, to use Matthew Arnold's phrase, that he sought always to be "the friend and aider of all who would live in the spirit." His purpose was not to *instill* truth, but rather to *release* it. His own comment on Goethe's place among the German Romantics describes perfectly his relationship to Thoreau and Whitman and even Melville: "He was the cow from which the rest drew their milk." Sufficient testimony to his continuing power to inspire and shape the thought and development of others is Spiller's moving declaration in this volume: "I would try to be the American Scholar. Emerson was to blame."

Not long after Emerson's first acquaintance with Thoreau he came to view his young friend, who had heard his stirring address "The American Scholar" during his senior year at Harvard, as potentially the free and talented American he had called for. Was he not versed in books, responsive to nature, fit for doing as well as thinking? Emerson respected his firm build, his strong and useful hands, his brain meshed beautifully with his capacity for action. Here was a body and mind and independent spirit perfectly fitted for the task of establishing a new and original relationship with nature.

Thoreau's responses to such challenges were immediate and dramatic. He perceived clearly the meaning of America. It was an opportunity for new beginnings. "The Atlantic is a Lethean stream, in our passage over which we have an opportunity to forget the Old World and its corrupted institutions." Lewis Mumford describes Thoreau's particular Americanism in terms of his response to his natural environment. He credits him with accepting, as the early pioneer had not, the challenge to meet "the expectation of the land," and of thus helping precipitate "the dawn" of "the golden Day" in American experience and culture. To these ends *Walden*, as well as most of Thoreau's other writing, is addressed directly to his fellow Americans. His first stand is taken against a crass and corrupting materialism that stifles all truly charitable impulse in man and blinds him to the loveliness of surrounding nature; his less fortunate fellows and the gracious land itself become the chief objects of his exploitation. This is the lower economy; Thoreau would call his fellows to follow the higher economy of charity in human relationships and the joyous perception of the beauty of the natural world. Puritanism, Thoreau laments, "has hung its harp on the willows, and cannot sing a song in a strange land. It has dreamed a sad dream, and does not yet welcome the morning with joy." In contrast he offers his own creed. "If the day and the night are such that you greet them with joy, and life emits a fragrance like flowers and sweet-scented herbs, is more elastic, more starry, more immortal—that is your success." Shanley pursues this line of thought, calling Thoreau a *sensuous ascetic*.

If Thoreau's Americanism and art seem grounded primarily in his original responses to the natural world in which he found himself, Whitman's, in contrast, seem to spring out of his deep involvement in the development of fresh human relationships and institutions appropriate to the New World. One thinks immediately of his comment on the gestation of *Leaves of Grass*. It was not, he said, "in the usual way of an author withdrawing, composing his work in a study, addressing himself to the literary formulation, consulting authorities, and the like, but in the way of first merging oneself in all the living flood and practicality and fervency of that period. Only after such contact with all common aspects of society is it just possible that there comes to a man, a woman, the divine power to speak words." How beautifully this describes his belief and what he would like always to practice. I was somewhat startled during a recent visit with Stovall when he remarked, quite flatly, "As a matter of fact Whitman cared little for English poetry, or poetry of any kind, either before or after 1855, though he was much interested in the lives of poets. He was too much absorbed with his own experience, particularly as it pertained to things American." And, Stovall continued, "the poems I love most, such as 'Out of the Cradle Endlessly Rocking' and 'When Lilacs Last in the Dooryard Bloom'd' were the products of deep feeling, half-conscious, rather than conscious artistic skill." These themes are pursued in Stovall's recent book *The Foreground of Leaves of Grass*, a fine study of Whitman, to which his essay in this collection might be considered a kind of epilogue.

Whitman repeatedly warns us of approaching his poetry by way of aesthetic considerations mainly; the implications are that its shaping influences are to be found primarily in his deeply felt patriotic commitment. At any rate, he remained incapable of writing the poetry of *Leaves of Grass* until he had begun to express himself without regard for literary forms or aesthetic authority. The way was risky, and he knew it. But as we look back over his entire life and career, he seems right in his approach; given his background, and time, and place, and temperament, there was simply no other way for achieving precisely what he did. We marvel that a thing done so timidly and falteringly, once accomplished, could seem so bold and grand.

But, as *Democratic Vistas* makes abundantly clear, Whitman sometimes feared the inadequacy of mere political institutions and the deceptive charms of American materialism. He sees that true democracy depends upon a certain condition of mind and spirit, for which literature must assume the responsibility, and calls the American poet to the task of infusing the national life with spirituality and beauty, with grace and commitment.

Nowhere is such patriotic commitment on the part of Melville more eloquently expressed than in his remarkable review of Hawthorne's *Mosses from an Old Manse.* It was the convergence of his considerations of the problems of his American materials and his own deep-seated Americanism, of his profound reading of Shakespeare, and of his immediate excitement over a renewed discovery of Hawthorne at a crucial moment in his own literary development, that makes his review of a book of short stories one of the most creative bits of nonfictional prose of his period. Howard explores this experience in depth and with new insights in his essay, especially as it relates to the influence of Shakespeare on *Moby-Dick.*

My particular interest here is in the convergence of the shaping forces already pointed out and in the great outburst of Melville's patriotic fervor, his Americanism, which it precipitates. Following that outburst and speculation about the possibility of an American Shakespeare and high praise of Hawthorne, come two highly indicative statements. First, "You must have plenty of searoom to tell the Truth in; especially when it seems to have an aspect of newness, as America did in 1492." And second, the declaration, "However great may be the praise I have bestowed upon Hawthorne, I feel that in so doing I have served and honored myself, more than him." These two statements bring into focus what has been at work all along, it seems to me. The power and ultimate significance of this essay resides in the fact that, consciously or unconsciously, Melville is writing of himself, and within a framework that has so objectified his own struggle and growth that he can pour out otherwise untold secrets freely and with grace and beauty. There is no better guide to the well-springs of Melville's literary genius than this remarkable document. And his own American character lies at the core.

When we see that Ahab, on at least one level of meaning, is highly suggestive of the rugged individualists, the strong-willed captains of industry, who, at the public expense, were so rapidly transforming the country and the age, we realize that Melville's Americanism, in contrast to Whitman's, frequently takes the form, not of celebration, but rather of tragic evaluation of that exuberant and pervasive spirit of individualism in whose name so many dubious activities were justified as the earthly revelation of a providential design. But this is not the whole story; Melville's attitude toward the American dream is always richly ambiguous. In *Moby-Dick* he can be as rhapsodic as Emerson or Whitman in praising the dignity of every man, no matter how humble. "But this august dignity I treat of, is not the dignity of kings and robes, but that abounding dignity which has no robed investiture. Thou shalt see it shining in the arm that wields a pick or drives a spike; that democratic dignity which, on all hands, radiates without end from God! Himself! The great God absolute! The center and circumference of all democracy! *His* omnipresence, *our divine equality*."

But the darker voice of Melville, it seems to me, is the more characteristic voice as he tends to isolate himself from the rhythm and tempo of a time about which he had grave misgivings. Be that as it may, his spiritual isolation always occurred in a specific American context. Fighting at times to free himself from his nation, he had to keep his nation in his art. As Jay Hubbell so wisely states it in his recent book *Who Are the Major American Writers?*, "Melville, even in his darkest moods, was a great writer who in reality had no desire to be regarded as an alien in his own country."

As a writer, Melville never doubted that great themes could be created out of the common stuff of American life. In fact, he demonstrated how it could be done. He was in the broadest sense a patriot who deeply distrusted certain aspects of the American variety of idealism around him. For every trans-cendental illusion, he felt disillusion; but he could not shake free from the idea that this land might yet live up to its prom-ise. Like all of the transcendentalists, Melville was a demo-crat; but his democracy sprang rather from his sympathies and experiences than from his philosophy, and for that very reason is frequently more effectively and gracefully written into his fiction than it is written by any of his contemporaries into their transcendental essays. His experience before the mast had been traumatic at times, but it taught him a deep sympathy for the common man. He could fear for the future of that common man, even in a professedly democratic land. It is probably not going too far to say that his democracy grew out of his pessimism; certainly its origins were not in any transcendent faith in the divinity of man. The conclusion of Howard's essay speaks cogently to this point.

But if it was Melville's early life before the mast that de-mocratized his spirit, it was that life also that provided solid foundations for his thoroughly Americanized literary form and style. Those foundations consisted of folklore, and popu-lar theater, and frontier humor and exaggeration, and Ameri-can rhetoric and oratory. Melville loved all of these and in *Moby-Dick* we have the most extensive use of folklore to be found anywhere in our literature. As he says, the *Acushnet* was his Yale and Harvard, and he never lost the full flavor of

Preface

the folklore that pulsed through him in the sophisticated processes of formal schooling. Furthermore he delighted in folklore, the *very bloodstream of humanity* he called it. Tales and skits and songs were the delight of every dog-watch aboard the Nantucket whalers and the best of them stayed with Melville. On such foundations he gradually shaped a style distinctly American: large in idea, expansive, forceful, fresh, picturesque, vivid in imagery and free-flowing in humor; one of its chief charms is its freedom from all scholastic rules and conventions.

In this volume we have taken our bicentennial as an occasion for considering the nature of the American character and for paying tribute to four major American writers who as dedicated patriots continue to help us understand its origins and implications. We have also explored their Americanism as a shaping force in their art. Four of our most distinguished American scholars have joined forces in the continuing process of periodically reclaiming a heritage that must be kept alive because it continues to be eminently usable and nourishing to our people and our artists.

Thomas Edward Crawley
Hurt Professor of English
Hampden-Sydney College

Acknowledgments

As director of the year's exploration of our cultural heritage, culminating in our literary symposium and the publication of these essays, I would like to express my personal indebtedness, as well as that of the College at large, to the Board of Trustees for making the necessary funds available for a full and exciting program and to three members of the College faculty and staff—Sandra Keys, Virginia Redd, and John Brinkley—for their competent and always cheerful assistance. I would also like to recognize the major contributions made by four of my students who held Ropp Research Fellowships in English: Jeffrey Lynn, Richard Young, Mark Burris, and Mark Lee. We are all grateful to Professors Howard, Shanley, Spiller, and Stovall, not only for their lectures, but also for their graciousness in making themselves available to our students. In addition, Professor Stovall gave invaluable aid in helping plan the symposium and acting as its coordinator. Finally, and most important of all, I wish to acknowledge the contribution made by Charles M. Guthridge of the Class of 1968 in serving as Vice Chairman of the Hampden-Sydney Bicentennial Committee, Chairman of the Sub-committee on America's Cultural Heritage, and President of the Alumni Association. He provided the imaginative, and yet practical, leadership making the full achievement of our goals possible. Through his sensitivity and commitment to the academic ideals of the college and his enthusiastic personal participation in all of the special events of the 1974–1975 academic year, he has written his name large in the annals of his Alma Mater.

T.E.C.

FOUR MAKERS OF THE
AMERICAN MIND

THE FOUR FACES OF EMERSON

Robert E. Spiller

The purpose of this conference, as Dr. Crawley states it, is to arrive at a better understanding of "the American character as reflected and/or projected in the writings of Emerson, Thoreau, Whitman and Melville," and it is my assignment to open the discussion with some reflections on the way Ralph Waldo Emerson contributed to shaping that American national character.

There is some logic in this plan for, by 1850, Emerson certainly stood at the center of American cultural and intellectual life as the spokesman for that confidence in the integrity of the individual which inspired Whitman to write *Leaves of Grass* and has inspired all of us as Americans since to carry the message of freedom and the rights of man to the oppressed and enslaved peoples of the earth. What could be more centrally American than that passage in the essay "Self-Reliance" which we all know: "Trust thyself; every heart vibrates to that iron string. . . . Great men have always done so . . . and we are now men, guides, redeemers, and benefactors, obeying the Almighty effort and advancing on Chaos and Dark."

Somehow we as a nation seem to have absorbed from the zeal of the early settlers and the great documents of the Revolutionary period the conviction that we, like the Israelites, are a chosen people with a mission to right the wrongs of the past and to teach the lessons of the future. Even at this late day, I for one have donned uniform to cross the Atlantic in order

3

"to make the world safe for democracy" and I have spent much of my professional life shaping American studies programs here and in Europe and Asia in the conviction that America has something special to say to the world.

Surely then, when Paul Elmer More, as late as 1917, says in the *Cambridge History of American Literature*, "It becomes more and more apparent that Emerson, judged by an international or even by a broad national standard, is the outstanding figure of American letters," we might expect to learn from him the message of which we are to be the missionaries. But perhaps we should pause, because this is the man who once took as his motto: "A great man is he who answers questions which I have not skill to put." Emerson was a humble seeker after a truth he never fully found and not the Delphic oracle that Whitman thought him. Perhaps we look to him rather because he confronted the confused complexity that our national experience really is and learned a way—not to solve its problems or to preach its message—but to live with it and inwardly to reflect its diverse character.

In this paper I will be speaking on three levels. The first is the obvious one, the experience and teachings of Ralph Waldo Emerson as he passed through the four stages of life from youth to maturity and presented, as we have recently come to recognize, four quite different faces to the world. First he appeared as the young idealist attacking the strongholds of tradition; then as the cosmic sage rising above the battle and maintaining an easy calm of untried authority; then we discovered beneath this surface the disturbed seeker facing the essential tragic issues of life without revealing his distress; and finally he appeared as the wise man who had discovered a balanced way of life for himself and for others in a suspended dualism of the ideal and the real.

The second level of my thinking runs parallel with this but will only be hinted at. It is the level of my own personal lifelong intimacy with Emerson's evolving thought and feeling as I leaned on him in my own progress through much the same curve of life; and the third level—which is more speculative and unprovable even though it is the subject of this conference —the concentration of the whole American experience in the intuitive subconscious of this puzzling man. Mine will be the message of the Devil's advocate. I will be trying to explain why I and Emerson the American Isaiah and the American people themselves seem often to have failed because they asked the right but the unanswerable questions.

You will be hearing more about Whitman later but I must take him as my springboard because he represented the obvious confident external American man, whereas Emerson was the perplexed and searching prophet of the inner national consciousness. He was, as the psycho-historian Erik Erikson has recently portrayed Jefferson in his book *Dimensions of a New Identity*, equally the representative American man and an index to the inner national character.

Jefferson, Dr. Erikson believes, had to rediscover a sense of identity by becoming "at one with myself" and at the same time establishing his affinity with a new world community's "sense of being at one with its future as well as its history." He achieved this by being a man "centered in a true identity" but able like Proteus to assume a variety of roles or faces behind which his true self could hide, and thus lead the early Americans in their "job of developing an American character out of the regional and generational polarities and contradictions of a nation of immigrants and migrants." The true American is not that written into the Constitution; he is a multi-ethnic mass of restless, seeking, ever-moving humanity in a vast undeveloped continent.

Even though Whitman declared himself the disciple of Emerson as the cosmic heart of man and the voice of the American people, there was little sympathetic exchange be-

tween the two poets after the first overenthusiastic response
of the latter to *Leaves of Grass* in 1855. Although they could
compete equally for the role of the man most representative
of the American national character in the mid-nineteenth
century, they were at opposite poles of feeling, thought, and
action. What we can learn about the American from Emerson
may supplement but it does not repeat what we can learn
about him from Whitman, or Thoreau, or Melville. Whereas Whitman thought himself the voice of the common man—
the democratic mass of humanity—and of the westward moving frontier, Emerson spoke only the message of that inner
frontier of mind and heart which was shaping the experience
of a new man in a new world. In 1855, when he greeted Whitman "at the beginning of a great career," Emerson, who was
only sixteen years his senior, was nearing the end of a distinguished career of his own. He had delivered his last important course of lectures on "The Conduct of Life" four years
before, and he was preparing his last wholly original book,
English Traits, for the press. Truly this was the watershed
of the romantic movement in American literature!

Emerson was descended in an almost unbroken line from
the liberal branch of the theological establishment of New
England. Born in 1803 of a father who was minister of the
First Church of Boston and one of the founders of the Unitarian schism, and of a mother who was descended in a direct
line from the Reverend Peter Bulkeley, one of the founders of
Concord, he had little choice of his role in life. One of four
boys, he was brought up by his pious and thrifty mother
after his father's death in 1811, educated at the Boston Latin
School and Harvard College, and ordained in 1829 at the
Second Unitarian Church in Boston, where he officiated until
his resignation three years later. In those few years he lived
a full and promising life. Married to a beautiful and delicate
girl and minister of a prominent church, he preached over a

hundred sermons that showed the strength of his critical mind and the radical questioning of all formulated doctrine. Then, in 1831–32, the whole structure of his life collapsed. His wife died, he resigned from his charge because his conscience would not allow him to administer the sacrament of the Holy Communion as a ritual regardless of his personal feelings at any given time, and he set out alone for Europe in quest of a more open and free base for his developing transcendental beliefs. On his return the next year, he was invited by his cousin George, a leader in the new Lycaeum Movement, to deliver a lecture on science, and a new career as itinerant public lecturer opened before him.

The moment of revelation had come to him in the botanical garden in Paris. "The universe is a more amazing puzzle than ever," he wrote in his journal after this experience. "As you look along the bewildering series of animated forms, the hazy butterflies, the carved shells, the birds, beasts, insects, fish,— and the upheaving principle of life everywhere incipient, in the very rock aping organized forms . . . . I am moved by strange sympathies. I will listen to the invitation. I will be a naturalist."

In this doctrine of the exact but mysterious correspondence of the law of nature with the law of God, Emerson had discovered the "First Philosophy" which was to be his substitute for creed for the rest of his life, and an open approach to truth which was to take the place of all systems of received doctrine. When he moved to Concord in 1834 and married Lydia Jackson the next year, he was ready to rebuild his life on the foundations of his own intuitive but fluent convictions.

The first face of the new Emerson is therefore that of a confident and enthusiastic young reformer, driven by his own spirit of independence to defy all truth that rested only on authority and to construct his own message to the world on the truth received directly from intuition and personal experience.

The new testament of his faith was the little book *Nature*, conceived on the boat when returning from Europe in 1833 and published three years later, a poem and a guide to life in the prose of revelation rather than of logic. Meanwhile he had been lecturing regularly on the literature and the leaders of thought of the past; now, with his testament in hand, he was ready for a frontal attack on the two entrenched establishments of his own intellectual and moral world: the academic of Harvard College, and the theological of the Divinity School. The twin orations of 1837 and 1838 were the result. After them, he stood alone, a new man in a new world of the mind, Adam born again of the inner life.

At this point, what I have so far said and what I plan to say becomes for me a curious mixture of my subject with my own spiritual and intellectual autobiography, for I discovered the Emerson of *Nature* back in my college days of 1914–17 when I threw aside my Episcopal upbringing and my formal schooling to explore the worlds of history, art, literature, and religion in the classroom and in the minds of like curious friends and teachers. Then, after a year in Europe (courtesy of Uncle Sam), I returned to build my own world of the mind in a new and personal commitment to the basic law of self-discovery. Leaving the security of the great university, I chose to teach in a small Quaker college to pick the subjects I needed for the freedom to build my own career. You know the result. Ultimately I came to apply the same principle of integrity to the literary history of my own country that I had found so necessary for myself. I had been taught to think of American as a branch of English literature; I now recognized it as the voice of a culture which had evolved from the impact of ancient civilizations on a primitive environment. It must be studied anew from the roots up. I would try to be the American Scholar. Emerson was to blame.

With that, I will leave the personal and return to my subject; but perhaps I have let you in on a secret which will help you to understand why Emerson—at least for me—is the epitome of the American national character, and why, when we came to the point in planning *Literary History of the United States* at which we chose the chapters that each of us wanted to write ourselves, I said, "Give me Emerson and you can deal out the rest."

Emerson appears first to us then in the role of the newborn poet of Nature, eager to rediscover himself and his place in the universe, forsaking the past, challenging the present, reaching out to the future. "Standing on the bare ground— my head bathed by the blithe air and uplifted into infinite space—all mean egotism vanishes. I become a transparent eyeball; I am nothing; I see all; the currents of the Universal Being circulate through me; I am part or parcel of God."

The little book *Nature* which he offered in 1836 had been composed with great care. The task of formulating the new philosophy was one of discovering and defining the place of the self in the cosmic universe where the moral law (the law of God) above was as a mirror to the natural law below, re-flecting the truth in a one-to-one relationship at every point.

Emerson had at first planned two books, each dealing with a way of bringing these two together into a realization of what it meant to be. The self could look down to nature and find there the reflection of God, or it could look upward and in-ward to "the ineffable essence which we call spirit, . . . the organ through which the universal spirit speaks to the indi-vidual. . . . Idealism sees the world in God." The mirror re-versed—. The first of these books was to be called *Nature*, the second *The Soul*. In the end the two were merged into one, in a rising and falling action which keeps forever fluent within each individual self the ever-changing, ever the same, relationship between God and the world about us.

"Philosophically considered," Emerson first declares, "the

universe is composed of Nature and the Soul. Strictly speaking, therefore, all that is separate from us, all which Philosophy distinguishes as the NOT ME, that is, both nature and art, all other men and my own body, must be ranked under the name NATURE, ... the essences unchanged by man, space, the air, the river, the leaf, ... as well as the mixture of [man's] will with the same things, as in a house, a canal, a statue, a picture." For Emerson there are four ways in which God is revealed in these things: Commodity, or daily use; Beauty, or the pleasure in contemplation of form and color; Language, or the symbols by which natural facts become spiritual facts; and Discipline, or the power of Reason which perceives and teaches "the analogy that marries Matter and Mind." Once having risen by these means to the plane of the Ideal, the self can be expressed in science, in poetry, in religion—an unending process of teaching and learning.

With his ideological platform thus firmly laid and his tools in hand, the young Emerson was ready to accept the invitation of the Phi Beta Kappa Society of Harvard to deliver its annual address in August of 1837. His subject was assigned, and many learned discourses had been delivered in past years expounding the varieties and the virtues of academic scholarship. It was a time to announce and to discuss the learning of the past and its authority in the present.

"I accept this topic," Emerson began in his usual low key, "*The American Scholar.* Year by year we come up hither to read one more chapter of his biography. Let us inquire what light new days and events have thrown on his character and his hopes." So far there was probably no stir in his robed and sober audience; but then he threw his challenge. The scholar, he announced, is the delegated intellect of a living society: "In the right state he is *Man Thinking.* In the degenerate state, when the victim of society, he tends to become a mere thinker, or still worse, the parrot of other men's thinking." He must use—not merely absorb and pass on—the tools of scholarship: nature, or the world about; books, or the record of the past; and action, or the vocabulary of the present.

Bliss Perry has given us a graphic account of what happened when faculty and students filed out. The repercussions of that moment are felt in the halls of Academe down to the present day.

No less stunning was the second occasion when the students of the Divinity School invited him to address them the next year. One would hardly expect a minister of the radical branch of the New England faith—albeit he had resigned from his own church—to attack Unitarianism in its own stronghold. But the young challenger was unflinching. Received and formulated doctrine, however liberal, could not take the place of a living and functioning Christian life. "Historical Christianity," he said, "has fallen into the error that corrupts all attempts to communicate religion . . . it is not the doctrine of the soul, but an exaggeration of the personal, the positive, the ritual. It has dwelt, it dwells, with noxious exaggeration about the *person* of Jesus. The soul knowns no person."

Here was heresy—inexcusable, not to be forgiven. But Emerson clung to his new-found faith in life as function rather than fact, as relation rather than as fixed truth. He faced the lonely path ahead.

With platform as well as pulpit becoming less and less available for his message, he now turned to the printed page. An avid reader of Montaigne and Bacon, the thought came to him that, by cutting, compressing, arranging, and refining the thought he had by now expressed in several series of subscription lectures in the Masonic Temple of Boston and elsewhere, he could perhaps offer a volume of moral essays. By 1841 the project had been completed and the first series of *Essays* appeared in Boston and London.

The effect was almost instantaneous and the young radical

became the cosmic sage. Emerson's second face—behind the mask of print—became that of the wise philosopher, the assured teacher, the secular saint.

But the essays themselves are very difficult to read, a fact which has often worried me as I have leapt from one brilliant phrase to the next but plodded through the long paragraphs which seemed to lead nowhere. The difficulty, I think, lies in Emerson's method of thinking rather than in the complexity of his thought. He was intuitive rather than logical; and language, as he explains himself, was for him the symbol of spiritual insights rather than the conveyer of ideas and facts. His style is still that of the spoken sermon or lecture, even though disciplined by that of the epigrammatic Bacon. Throughout his mature life he kept a journal in which he deposited the nuggets that he dug from the earth of reading and experience—his "savings bank," he called it. His method of composition was first to choose a theme—Self-Reliance, the Over-Soul, Compensation, Love, History—and then to build around it, as a musician might a symphony, a composition made up of the *notes* (the pun is inescapable) he gleaned from his own written words, playing the strings against the woodwinds, the treble over the base, as counterpoint and harmony lead his fugue on through circles of motion to its own climax. To hear a lecture or to read an essay by Emerson is a listening experience of the inner sensibilities rather than a logical exercise of the mind.

Almost all of "Self Reliance" for example is made up of phrases, sentences, and paragraphs taken from the various journals—some of them as early as 1832 or 1833—and the courses of lectures he had delivered to winter audiences in Boston between 1837 and 1840, themselves composed in the same way largely of journal passages. Yet Emerson wrote, even after the critical success of his *Essays* in England, "I shall someday write something better than those poor cramped

arid 'Essays' which I almost hate the sight of," and his revisions in the 1847 edition proves that he tried.

But the *Essays*, with their companion volume of three years
later, constitute one of the major classics of American literature; for their tone is that of mature authority as they open
and close the doors of the spirit, even though their author in
the final essay protests, "Let me remind the reader that I am
only an experimenter, . . . an endless seeker with no Past at
my back." He might have added, "I am the shaper of the new
American gospel, I am the voice of my people and my time."
Whether he would or not, his doctrines of the centrality of the
single self, the all-presence of a pervading over-soul or God,
the correspondence of the moral and the natural worlds, and
the balanced duality of experience became the creed of a new
faith, and the youthful protester took on the robes of the
cosmic seer, robes which, to the public mind at least, he was
never able to get free of.

Is it stretching the analogy too far to see in Emerson's protests against conformity to the rigid structure of a present
based on inherited authority and his vigorous assertion of the
right of the individual soul to live its own life a parallel to the
Declaration of Independence, the war of the Revolution, and
the founding of a new nation in a new world? And, to carry
the analogy further, can we find in his efforts to formulate his
own "First Philosophy" and to set himself up as lecturer on
moral fundamentals and individual rights a parallel to the
making of the Constitution, the Monroe Doctrine, and the
opening of the West? The Napoleonic wars and the subse-
quent waves of revolution that spread throughout Europe in
1830 and 1848 were open invitations to the confident new
nation to prove itself by internal expansion and consolidation
and by carrying the messages of democracy and human rights
to the rising peoples of Europe. The American constitution
became in the first half of the century a model for the political

liberation and reform of the Old World, and caused the first major waves of the migration of the oppressed peoples of Ireland, Germany, and Italy to assault the harbors of the Atlantic and to push across the plains.

Can we now see Emerson as the philosopher, the interpreter, the representative man of the American national character in the first stages of its formulation? At least for the purposes of this conference may I propose such a thesis as an acceptable hypothesis if not quite a historical fact? And can we keep this analogy in mind as I return my focus to Emerson the man and his spiritual life, without making it too specific point for point? And may I also remember, without bothering you with the details, how during my own twenty-four years at Swarthmore I established my own professional and personal orientation to a society rediscovering itself after its first World War, weathering a depression, and gradually taking its place as one of the major world powers? Whether you share this three-level thinking with me or not, I am having fun with it inside myself as I talk.

But to return to Emerson, now settled in the big white Coolidge house on the Lexington Road, building his family, gathering his circle of friends, and stimulating the agencies of the so-called Transcendental Movement: the *Dial* magazine, the experimental agricultural community Brook Farm, and the informal Transcendental Club.

The third face of Emerson should have worn the firm mouth, the wise reserve, the confident eyes of a life achieved and quietly lived, and so it seemed to him and his family and friends when, in December 1840, he wrote to George Ripley of his decision not to join Brook Farm: "The ground of my decision is almost purely personal to myself. . . . That which determines me is the conviction that the Community is not good for me. While I see it may hold out many inducements for others it has little to offer me which with resolution

I cannot procure for myself. . . . It seems to me a circuitous and operose way of relieving myself of any irksome circumstances which I ought to take on myself" (Let. II, 325). Thus committed to Concord and to himself at the age of thirty-five, he settled with his growing family into the comfortable home in which, forty-two years later, in 1882, he died.

But the image which he thus assumed of the philosopher-friend was deceptive because, as Stephen Whicher has pointed out in his "inner life" of Emerson, *Freedom and Fate*, the period between 1839 and at least 1844 was actually one of storm and stress equal almost to anything a Byron or a Goethe might experience, but storm and stress held firmly in control.

The strain perhaps began with the death of his beloved brother Charles in 1836, followed by that of his infant son and namesake Waldo in 1842, but the center of tension was inward and not in external events. The Divinity School address of 1839 was his last unqualified statement of enthusiastic idealism, and its reception was devastating to his personal sense of security. Andrews Norton, then the most powerful presence in the Unitarian fold, wrote a systematic and vicious personal attack in *A Discourse on the Latest Form of Infidelity* in the same year, and a factional war of which Emerson was both the cause and the silent center broke out. "Who are these murmurers, these haters, these revilers?" he asked in his Journal. "In the present droll posture of my affairs, when I see myself suddenly raised into the importance of a heretic, I am very uneasy. . . . I shall go on just as before, seeing whatever I can and telling what I see." But his self-confidence had been deeply shaken. "Steady, steady! When the fog of good and evil affection falls, it is hard to see and walk straight."

Perhaps he was speaking of his own efforts at recovery when, in the poem "Uriel," probably written later, he called the challenge of the young God Uriel a "lapse."

15

> Line in nature is not found;
> Unit and Universe are round;
> In vain produced, all rays return:
> Evil will bless and ice will burn. . . .

And when he had spoken thus,

> A sad self-knowledge, withering, fell
> On the beauty of Uriel; . . .
> And a blush tinged the upper sky,
> And the gods shook, they knew not why.

"Circles," included in the first volume of *Essays*, revealed the same shift from the bold egotism of the Addresses to an acceptance of the principle of learning through an ever-expanding experience. "The eye is the first circle; the horizon which it forms is the second; and throughout nature this primary figure is repeated without end. . . . There are no fixtures in nature. The universe is fluid and volatile. Permanence is but a word of degrees. . . . Do not set the least value on what I do, or the least discredit on what I do not as if I pretended to settle anything as true or false. I unsettle all things. . . . I simply experiment, an endless seeker with no past at my back." "Yes," he is still saying, "trust thyself—even when in the deepest doubt."

The summer of 1841 was apparently the nadir of his spirits. Invited to address the undergraduate literary society at Colby College in Maine, he found it impossible to pull his old thoughts on Nature together again into a coherent statement. Borrowing ideas heavily from articles in the *Encyclopaedia Americana* and elsewhere, and on his own recent and miscellaneous entries in his Journals, he paced the beach at Nantasket where he had gone alone or sought solace in his study. "The Method of Nature" contains some of his best passages but is confused and unconvincing. The fact that his next series of Boston lectures on "The Times" dealt critically with both "The Conservative" and "The Transcendentalist" suggests that he was going through a period of self-analysis and reappraisal of his identity and his deepest convictions.

Committed initially to the doctrine of Transcendentalism, which required that one live by the higher moral law, he was learning the hard way that the doctrine of correspondence between the moral and the natural law on which it was based simply does not work from day to day. In three areas of his private life also he was facing the tragic issue of all time—the realization that what must be, can't be: the areas of money, women, and social concerns.

Although he had a small inheritance from his first wife, the panic of 1837 made the Boston lecture series essential, and when income from these began to dwindle, he responded to the lure of the Lycaeum Movement more and more and began to go on lecture tours, first to neighboring New England towns, then to New York and Philadelphia, and finally to England and to the West. His English friend Thomas Carlyle not ineptly called him "the lonely wayfaring man" as he came to spend more and more time away from home.

He was also discovering that Plato was wrong about friendship, especially with women. The vigorous Margaret Fuller and the starry-eyed Caroline Sturgis, as well as others, became increasingly embarrassing as the close relationships that Transcendentalism encouraged became dangerously absorbing. This is a whole story in itself, which can now be more fully told as suppressed letters come to light, but this is probably not the place to go into details, however intriguing. Suffice it that any man who allows his friendships for three or four women at the same time to threaten to cross the line into love may be headed for a nervous breakdown or worse.

And finally, the issue of social involvement, to which I have already referred in the Brook Farm incident and Emerson's decision to go it alone. The first real evidence of a shift of emphasis toward social concern had appeared in his Boston lecture of 1839–40 on "The Present Age" and the omission of the series altogether in 1840–41; but in January of that year he made his first overt statement on social concerns in the lecture to the Mechanics Apprentices' Library Association in Boston on "Man the Reformer."

But it was the slavery question which finally broke down his resistance. As the Abolitionist Movement began to heat up in the thirties, the slavery question had forced itself more and more on literary idealists like Whittier, Lowell, and Emerson. How could the ownership of a fellow human being be reconciled with the basic American doctrines of individual integrity and the rights of man? The answer is that it could not be. Here was the major public challenge to Transcendentalism and the moral law. Whittier and Lowell were easy converts, but Emerson was slower. When he did go over it was to declare, not only against slavery as such but against social evils in general, and the third of his stages of development began to take on a different emphasis with his frontal attack on trade as the cancer of modern society in his 1841 lecture on "Man the Reformer." Even so, it was slavery which finally brought him into the open as the nearest thing to an activist that he ever became. He had been shocked by the murderous attack on the Abolitionist printer Lovejoy in 1837 and he had read an address on slavery at the Concord Church at that time, but he still argued that the answer to social evil lay in the moral education of the individual rather than in concerted social action.

All three of these influences were of course contributory to his depressed state of mind in the third period, but the true core of it was inward and philosophical dismay which is perhaps best expressed in the essay on "Experience" in the second collection of his *Essays* in 1844. Here is perhaps the furthest

18

swing of the pendulum away from his early idealism and self-reliance. He had already stated in an elementary form in the earlier essay on "Compensation" the suspended dualism which was to become his final position. "Everything runs to excess," he concludes in the later essay; "every good quality is noxious if unmixed, and, to carry the danger to the edge of ruin, nature causes each man's peculiarity to superabound." Here for the first time he reached the conclusion that all of life is illusion and that temperament rather than self-reliance is the primary source of individualism. Illusion and Temperament are the first two "threads on the loom of time, these are the Lords of Life; the others are Succession, Surface, Surprise, Reality, Subjectiveness." All of life is relative in actual experience, determined by the quality and the mood of the individual in his special role and circumstance. Relativity and pragmatic acquiescence could hardly go further.

But by 1844, with the birth of his second son, Edward, and the publication of his second volume of *Essays*, Emerson may be said to have passed through what I like sometimes to call "middle-aged adolescence," the reorientation that happens to most people in middle life, and had his feet firmly on new ground. The fourth and mature face of Emerson was beginning to become more clear: the face of a poet-philosopher who had passed from idealism through skepticism into a pragmatic balance, a suspended dualism of irreconcilable opposites which provided both a way to dream and a way to live. To the unknowing, both in his time and in ours, the external calm of the Concord sage seemed unbroken; only those who could reach or listen carefully behind the serene mask and the controlled voice would find the restless flux of thought and feeling, the flow and ebb of life, the eternal questioning and searching that underlay the surface.

Representative Men, first delivered in 1845-46, read in England the following year, and published in 1850, may

19

well have been to some extent Emerson's answer to Carlyle's *Heroes and Hero Worship*. The Great Man, he insists, is not the unique and dominant leader who can impose himself on the masses; he is the best representative of a man's vocation at the highest point of its development, one kind of humanity at its best, like our old friend the scholar, who at his best is "man thinking." These are the men who came nearest to achieving a way of reaching closer to the ideal by best using the gifts which they had in excess but which are within the reach of all. The six Great Men chosen seem to be paired as opposites: Plato, the philosopher who excelled in intellect, is balanced by Swedenborg, the mystic who relied on intuitive insight; Montaigne, the skeptic who questioned all things, is set over against Shakespeare, who stood apart from life and accepted all, judged none; Napoleon, the man of the world who achieved through action, is countered by Goethe, the writer who reported the discoveries of the mind.

All of these Great Men failed to reach the ultimate goal of complete excellence; each revealed only one way to try and thereby offered a possible answer to the question of how to live in the real world while reaching for the ideal. Emerson was now engaged fully in his quest for an alternative to self-reliance.

He next turned from a consideration of the future of individuals to ask what kind of society is possible and acceptable when it deals realistically with existing facts and uses them in its search for the good life. The series of lectures which he delivered on his return from England and which he reworked into *English Traits* in 1856 is a thorough and critical analysis of a modern industrial-agricultural society, almost a portrait and a prediction of what American society could become.

Let me interrupt myself once again to remind you that we are thinking of Emerson as the spokesman for the American national character as well as for himself, and recall that at this time the nation was nearing its own tragic crisis of the Civil War. As it passed through this crisis and moved into a restless peace in which it attempted to rebuild its structure on a new and practical foundation without losing the dreams of the founders, so Emerson became more and more its spokesman, a man "centered in a true identity" but at the same time establishing his affinity with a new world community's "sense of being at one with its future as well as its history." As we approach our own time with its loss of security and identity, he seems more and more to become the representative American man in his relentless searchings rather than in his findings. He was the representative man of a new American national character, reflecting, as Erik Erikson pointed out, "the regional and generational polarities and contradictions of a nation of immigrants and migrants," which we most assuredly still are.

In the last of his major works, *The Conduct of Life*, lectures first delivered in 1851 and published in 1860, the balance between "Fate," or the "given" in life, and "Power," or the ability of man to use his resources productively, was struck. "Let us build altars," he asks, "to the Beautiful Necessity. Why should we fear to be crushed by savage elements, we who are made up of the same elements?" And again, "Who shall set a limit to the influence of a human being? . . . All power is of one kind, a sharing of the nature of the world." The dualism between Mind and Matter is still there, but somehow the order of priority has been reversed. It is in Matter—the laws of the new science—that one must first seek the shaping principle of life. "And so I think," he says in his lecture on "Worship," that the last lesson of life, the choral song which rises from all elements and all angels, is a voluntary obedience, a necessitated freedom. Man is made of the same atoms as the world is, he shares the same impressions, predispositions, and destiny. When his mind is illuminated, when his heart is kind, he throws himself joyfully into the sublime order, and does, with knowledge, what the stones do by structure." Such complete determinism was possible for the one-time young dreamer of the 1836 *Nature* because this statement was made three years before Darwin's *Origin of Species*, and the then current theory of evolutionary science allowed far more freedom of will and choice than later seemed possible under mechanistic science. Even though natural had superseded moral law as the prime shaper of the universe, the poet could still hold to the ultimate integrity of the individual soul.

"There is no chance and no anarchy in the universe," Emerson concludes. "All is system and gradation. Every god is there sitting in his sphere. The young mortal enters the hall of the firmament; there is he alone with them alone, they pouring on him benedictions and gifts, and beckoning him up to their thrones. On the instant, and incessantly, fall snowstorms of illusions. He fancies himself in a vast crowd which sways this way and that and whose movements and doings he must obey: he fancies himself poor, orphaned, insignificant. The mad crowd drives hither and thither, now furiously commanding this thing to be done, now that. What is he that he should resist their will, and think or act for himself? Every moment new changes and new showers of deceptions to baffle and distract him. And when, by and by, for an instant, the air clears and the cloud lifts a little, there are the gods still sitting around him on their thrones,—they alone with him alone."

This is the Emerson I have always known. For me, he is best enjoyed and used when I recall that he defined the American scholar as "Man Thinking" rather than as "a mere thinker." His is a "Philosophy of Living" in a scientifically determined world rather than a metaphysics, logic, or ethics. In the final analysis he is one of America's major poets, the recorder of the inward experience of a living present. As he has himself described his role: "The poet is representative. He stands among partial men for the complete man and apprises us not of his wealth, but of the common wealth."

THOREAU: HIS "LOVER'S QUARREL WITH THE WORLD"

J. Lyndon Shanley

Some years ago a whimsical scholar observed that many uninformed people thought Thoreau spent half of his life in jail, and the other half living at Walden Pond. More recently, many uninformed people adopted Thoreau as their patron saint because they saw him as an intransigent, antisocial, antigovernment rebel who had little or no respect for his country and its ideals; they read only his virulent denunciations of national and state actions in support of proslavery laws.

Thoreau was, indeed, a resigner and not a joiner; he was also an untiring critic of the status quo. But a careful consideration of his writings and deeds makes absolutely clear that, in spite of his lifelong quarrel with his world, he was a devout believer in ideals and hopes for the future on which the young nation depended: individual independence, individual self-perfection, and individual worth, and hopes for the future based on material and technological progress, and on the unspoiled natural world of the new land. He raised questions about these ideals and hopes from time to time only because he cared and thought about them so deeply. Some of his questions have not yet been answered.

J. Lyndon Shanley

I

In *Walden* the account of Thoreau's actual living at the pond begins: "When I took up my abode in the woods, that is, began to spend my nights as well as days there, which by accident, was on Independence Day. . . ." The "by accident" without comment is almost incredible for, certainly, no other day could have been so fitting a one for the intensely independent Thoreau to set out on a symbolic as well as actual adventure in independence. It is hard to understand why such a lover of symbols as Thoreau did not underline in *Walden* the relation of the Fourth of July to his first days of independence.

He knew very well how independent he wanted to be—he kept repeating in public and private, by act and by word, that he was his own man and nobody else's. You might say his life and writings were one long declaration of independence. One of his most humorous reports of himself was his answer to his Indian guide who asked him if he was a Protestant. "I did not at first know what to say, but I thought I could answer with truth that I was."

Neither employer, church, state, fellow townfolk, nor friends could force him. He would not do as others thought he should if he did not agree. When a school board member told him that he must physically punish his pupils in the public school, he arbitrarily selected several pupils and smacked them with a ferule—and then resigned. He "signed off" the church and filed a statement "I . . . do not wish to be regarded as a member of any incorporated society which I have not joined." If it had been feasible, he would have "signed off" the state. He did not pay his poll tax, first on the grounds of slavery, and then, later, also because of the Mexican War. For this he spent his famous night in jail. Another result was "Resistance to Civil Government" in which he dealt, forcefully, sometimes wildly, with the perennial problem of the

26

conflict between individual conscience and the power and will of the state. He would not be the servant or willing member of a government he thought wrong; he made clear how little he thought of his own. In his address "Slavery in Massachusetts," a burning attack on court action under the Fugitive Slave Law, he said, "My thoughts are murder to the State, and involuntarily go plotting against her." But in spite of the savage indignation here and in "A Plan for John Brown," he went about *his* business, for he wrote in his journal, "I do not think it is quite sane for one to spend his whole life in talking or writing about this matter [slavery], unless he is continuously inspired, and I have not done so. A man may have other affairs to attend to."

When he was thirty years old, he wrote to the secretary of his Harvard class, "I am a schoolmaster—a Private Tutor, a Surveyor—a Gardener, a Farmer—a Painter, I mean a House Painter, a Carpenter, a Mason, a Day-Laborer, a Pencil-Maker, a Glass-paper Maker, a Writer, and sometimes a Poetaster." In time he became surveyor-in-chief for Concord —but by no means did he work full-time. He was well aware that much more was expected of a graduate of Harvard College; he knew the judgment of many of his fellow townfolk; Emerson stated it later in his eulogy of Thoreau: ". . . instead of engineering for all America, he was the captain of a huckleberry party." In a contemporary phrase, Thoreau might have answered: "But what a huckleberry party!"

A journal note on his clothes, when he was forty years old, suggests the enduring conflict between Thoreau's choices and those of more conventional people in simple, everyday affairs. "Within a week I have had made a pair of corduroy pants, which cost when done $1.60. They have this advantage, that, beside being very strong, they will look about as well three months hence as now,—or as ill, some would say. Most of my friends are disturbed by my wearing them . . . others would not wear [corduroy], durable and cheap as it is, because it is worn by the Irish. Moreover, I like the color on other accounts. Anything but black clothes."

He did what he wanted to, as he would have all do what they wanted—he never ceased to insist that each one find *his* way; he wrote in *Walden*: "I would not have anyone adopt my mode of living on any account, . . . I desire that there may be as many different persons in the world as possible but I would have each one be very careful to find out and pursue his own way, and not his father's or his mother's or his neighbor's instead. The youth may build or plant or sail, only let him not be hindered from doing that which he tells me he would like to do." "If a man does not keep pace with his companions, perhaps it is because he hears a different drummer. Let him step to the music he hears, however measured or far away."

He demanded and took for himself no more than what he allowed and hoped for others; he *really* believed in independence. "I have been making pencils all day, and then at evening walked to see an old schoolmate who is going to help make the Welland Canal navigable for ships round Niagra[*sic*]. He cannot see any such motives and modes of living as I; professes not to look beyond the securing of certain 'creature comforts.' And so we go silently different ways, with all serenity, I in the still moonlight through the village this fair evening to write these thoughts in my journal, and he, forsooth, to mature his schemes to ends as good, maybe, but different. So are we two made, while the same stars shine quietly over us. If I or he be wrong, Nature yet consents placidly. She bites her lip and smiles to see how her children will agree. So does the Welland Canal get built, and other conveniences, while I live. Well and good, I must confess. Fast sailing ships are hence not detained."

But he did not always state the difference so serenely; more often he challenged his audience and readers as in *Walden*:

"The greater part of what my neighbors call good I believe in my soul to be bad, and if I repent of anything, it is very likely to be my good behavior [that is, what his neighbors would call good]. What demon possessed me that I behaved so *well?*" [Italics added.]

II

He challenged because of the high purpose he demanded of his fellow men to be as good as possible. He insisted everywhere and always: "Our whole life is startlingly moral. There is never an instant's truce between good and evil." All depended on the individual's courage and effort. "Whatever your sex or position, life is a battle in which you are to show your pluck, and woe be to the coward. . . . Despair and postponement are cowardice and defeat. Men were born to succeed, not fail."

And it was an unending battle as Thoreau had asserted early and late in his writings: "When I see a man with serene countenance in the sunshine of summer, drinking in peace in the garden or parlor, it looks like a great inward leisure that he enjoys; but in reality he sails on no summer's sea, but this steady sailing comes from a heavy hand on the tiller. . . . The man of principle gets never a holiday. Our true character silently underlies all our words and actions, as the granite underlines the other strata."

In the posthumously printed "Life without Principle" he declared that "the chief want, of every State [that he had] been into, was a high and earnest purpose in its inhabitants." And he wrote in his journal: "The constant inquiry which nature puts is: 'Are you virtuous? Then you can behold me.' Beauty, fragrance, music, sweetness, and joy of all kinds are for the virtuous." All individuals were to make themselves as good as possible, and not worry about others; what was essential was "that there should be some absolute goodness somewhere"; that would then affect all others. Thoreau's morality was demanding, but also bright. It implied a great faith in the individual.

As Paul Elmer More, a severe antiromantic critic put it: ". . . the freedom of the romantic school . . . in [Thoreau] . . . was for the practice of a higher self-restraint. Thoreau did actually violently break through the prison walls of routine, and yet kept a firm control of his career."

This endeavor was for the independent individual to exercise. Interference in others' lives Thoreau regarded as intolerable. The reformers and do-gooders of his day were anathemas to him. They were, he wrote in *Walden*, "Men of ideas instead of legs, a sort of intellectual centipede that made you crawl all over." And of three particular ones at his house: "They . . . rubbed you continually with the greasy cheeks of their kindness. . . . I was awfully pestered with one's benignity; feared I should get greased all over with it past restoration. . . . It was difficult to keep clear of his slimy benignity. . . ."

Nor would he have anything to do with the co-operative communities such as Brook Farm, Fruitlands, and the Hopedale Community, although they were founded to counteract, or to enable the individual to escape, the consequences of the new industrial life. "As for these communities," he wrote, "I think I had rather keep bachelor's hall in hell than go to board in heaven. Do you think your virtue will be boarded with? It will never live on the interest of your money, depend upon it. The boarder has no home. In heaven I hope to bake my own bread and clean my own linen. The tomb is the only boarding-house in which a hundred are served at once. In the catacomb we may dwell together and prop one another without loss."

No one could help in one's seeking to achieve, to develop the best one could be. Only from within oneself could come the flower and fragrance and fruit of the man that Thoreau wanted most: "how ... refreshing and encouraging ... would be fresh and fragrant thoughts communicated to us fresh and from a man's experience and life! I want none of his pity, nor sympathy, in the common sense, but that he should emit and communicate to me the essential fragrance, that he should not be forever repenting and going to church (when not otherwise sinning), but, as it were, going a-huckleberrying in the fields of thought, and enrich all the world with his visions and his joys."

III

Thoreau's passion for independence and his desire for moral perfection often led to deep disappointment with what he found in the world. Hence he was led to devastating comments on men and their ways. He told his fellow townsmen in his first lecture on his Walden experience: "It is very evident what mean and sneaking lives many of you live ... —lying, flattering, voting, contracting yourselves into a nutshell of civility, or dilating into an atmosphere of thin and vaporous generosity, that you may persuade your neighbor to let you make his shoes or his hat or his coat or his carriage or import his groceries for him."

"Good fellowship" he wrote in his Journal, "is commonly the virtue of pigs in a litter, which lie close together to keep each other warm." And another time: "A crowd of men seem to generate vermin even of the human kind. In great towns there is degradation undreamed of elsewhere,—gamblers, dog-killers, rag-pickers. Some live by robbery or luck." Men of manners were bad in a different way: "Nobody holds you more cheap than the men of manners. They are marks by the help of which the wearers ignore you and remain concealed themselves."

J. Lyndon Shanley

He was not an easy man to be with. One of his friends told Emerson, "I love Henry, but I cannot like him; and as for taking his arm, I should as soon think of taking the arm of an elm-tree." Hawthorne wrote in his Notebook that Emerson seemed to have suffered some discomfort when Thoreau lived in his house in 1842. "It may well be," Hawthorne commented, "that such a sturdy, uncompromising person is fitter to meet occasionally in the open air than as a permanent guest at table and fireside."

Too often only this difficult aspect of him is stressed. The whole man was far different. His interest in and sympathy for the ordinary, sometimes the extra- or sub-ordinary individual, reveal a man who believed (and behaved accordingly) that all sorts of men are valuable, not just as an act of other-worldly faith, but as a fact in this world.

He was a compassionate man; he cared most gently for a terrified runaway slave; he sympathized with and sometimes admired the poor, scorned, and mistreated Irish as they struggled with hunger and cold as well as ignorance. On occasion he wrote a letter for one of them, and on at least two occasions he raised money to help them. It would be difficult to find anything more tender and humane than his account in *Walden* of the weak minded pauper who visited his hut: "[He] expressed a wish to live as I did. He told me, with the utmost simplicity and truth, quite superior, or rather *inferior*, to anything that is called humility, that he was 'deficient in intellect.' These were his words. The Lord has made him so, yet he supposed the Lord cared as much for him as for another. 'I have always been so,' said he, 'from my childhood; I never had much mind; I was not like other children. I am weak in the head. It was the Lord's will, I suppose.' . . . in proportion as he appeared to humble himself was he exalted."

Thoreau was as democratic as he was humane. It was not the company and conversation of only his intellectual equals

32

and friends—Emerson, Alcott, Channing and others—that he sought. He appreciated and sought to know all kinds of men. "To-day, June 4th," he wrote in his journal, "I have been tending a burning in the woods. Ray was there. It is a pleasant fact that you will know no man long, however low in the social scale, however poor, miserable, intemperate, and worthless he may appear to be, a mere burden to society, but you will find at last that there is something which *he* understands and can do better than any other. I was pleased to hear that one man had sent Ray as the one who had had the most experience in setting fires of any man in Lincoln. He had experience and skill as a burner of brush." In July, Thoreau added: "It is astonishing how much information is to be got out of very unpromising witnesses. A wise man will avail himself of the observation of all."

And he did so. He was deeply curious about the simple wood-chopper, Therien; he wrote and rewrote the lengthy sketch of Therien in *Walden*: "He interested me because he was so quiet and solitary and so happy withal; a well of good humor and contentment which overflowed at his eyes. His mirth was without alloy. . . . In him the animal man chiefly was developed. In physical endurance and contentment he was cousin to the pine and the rock. . . . I asked him once, when I had not seen him for many months, if he had got a new idea this summer. 'Good Lord,' said he, 'a man that has to work as I do, if he does not forget the ideas he has had, he will do well. May be the man you hoe with is inclined to race; then by gorry, your mind must be there; you think of weeds.' . . . He suggested that there might be men of genius in the lowest grades of life, however permanently humble and illiterate, who take their own view always, or do not pretend to see at all; who are as bottomless even as Walden Pond was thought to be, though they may be dark and muddy."

On his last trip in the Maine woods, he made copious notes

on Joe Polis, his Indian guide: Joe's skill in canoeing, in hunting, in guiding himself in the woods, in making use of all materials at hand in woods; and his habits, and his opinions on Daniel Webster and education; and his outwitting of a very unecumenical priest; and his clear-headed sight of himself: "I suppose I live in New York, I be poorest hunter, I expect." Thoreau recorded all he could about this very different but capable and therefore interesting and valuable man.

He enjoyed Concord worthies such as George Minott, "perhaps the most poetical farmer" Thoreau knew, and Reuben Rice, who "had learned that rare art of living." But he also enjoyed simple laborers, icecutters, railroad men, woodcutters, and hunters and fishermen. His friend Ellery Channing told Sanborn that Thoreau was "Never in too much hurry for a dish of gossip, he could sit out the oldest frequenter of the barroom and was alive from top to toe with curiosity. . . . He did not end in this search [for knowledge] with farmers nor the broadcloth world; he knew another class of men, who hang on the outskirts of society, those who love grog and are never to be seen abroad without a fishpole or a gun in their hands. . . . I never knew him to go by this class without the due conversation. They had a sort of Indian or Gypsy life, and he loved to get this at second hand."

One of these was John Goodwin, who was considered a vicious character by most Concordians, but Thoreau was cheered by Goodwin's gathering driftwood and digging out stumps for his firewood; and in his journal he reported frequently on meetings with Goodwin, as he was fishing, trapping mink, shooting muskrats, when in the eyes of the respectable folk, he should have been earning his keep by laying walls. Thoreau recorded that Goodwin once sold a partridge he had shot during severe winter weather; when the buyer said the bird must have found it hard to get a living, Goodwin replied, "I guess she didn't find it any harder than I do."

George Melvin was another local ne'er-do-well, and Thoreau thanked his stars for "that Melvin who is such a trial to his mother." Melvin spent his time nutting, berrying, and hunting—and, as a trial to his mother, frequently drinking too much. One man hired him with the condition that Melvin not take his gun into the field. But, Thoreau reported, Melvin took his gun when his employer was away, and earned "two or three dollars with his game beside his day's work, but of course the last was neglected." Thoreau appreciated him because he spent his time in the woods and on the rivers and knew the countryside so well that he was able to show even Thoreau a flowering plant he had never seen before.

The essential quality of all these simple people was that they were themselves only and pretended to be no more. Thoreau cherished and enjoyed them for their simple and plain selves.

IV

Thoreau's democratic faith, hope, and charity in and for his fellow-men was firm, but his faith and hope in Progress, one of the idols of his day, wavered. He never lost faith and hope in the future, but he distrusted, indeed detested, some of the ways men were taking to it. For the wealth and luxuries that material and early technological progress produced he had no use at all: ". . . the rich man," he said, "is always sold to the institution which makes him rich." He wrote in *Walden* that "most of the luxuries, and many so-called comforts of life, are not only not indispensable, but positive hindrances to the elevation of mankind," and in his journal: "But may you not trace these stories of English comfort home to some wealthy Sardanapalus who was able to pay for obsequious attendance and for every luxury? How far does it describe merely the tact and selfishness of the wealthy class? Lord Somebody-or-other may have made himself comfortable, but the very style of his living makes it necessary that the great majority of his countrymen should be uncomfortable."

He watched the great increase of factories and the decrease of home industries with deep concern. He saw in the consequent division of labor a serious threat to a full, poetic, and rich life. Of his friend Rice, he wrote, "His life is poetic. He does the work himself. He combines several qualities and talents rarely combined." Of a boy happy in a woodchuck-skin hat made by his father, "Such should be the history of every piece of clothing that we wear." He observed: "To such a pass our civilization and division of labor has come that A, a professional huckleberry-picker, has hired B's field and . . . is now gathering the crop, perhaps with the aid of a patented machine; C, a professed cook, is superintending the cooking of the pudding made of some of the berries; while Professor D, for whom the pudding is intended, sits in library writing a book—a work on the Vaccinieae. . . . It will be worthless. There will be none of the spirit of the huckleberry in it. . . ."

But after visiting some gingham mills and learning the details of the way the cloth was made, he commented: "I am struck by the fact that no work has been shirked when a piece of cloth is produced. Every thread has been counted in the finest web. . . . The operator has succeeded only by patience, perseverance, and fidelity." The work was good; Thoreau objected only to the fact that the final end was money. He wrote in *Walden*: "I cannot believe that our factory system is the best way by which men may get clothing . . . as far as I have heard or observed, the principal object is, not that mankind may be well and honestly clad, but, unquestionably, that the corporation may be enriched."

His attitudes toward commerce were at odds. So far as it was for money, for luxuries, so far it was harmful. "There are certain current expressions and blasphemous moods of viewing things, as when we say 'he is doing a good business,' more prophane than cursing and swearing. There is death and sin in such words. Let not the children hear them." Of the California gold rush, he wrote in "Life without Principle," "I know of no more startling development of the immorality of trade, and all the common modes of getting a living."

But Thoreau also admired commerce as a brave enterprise of men exchanging goods around the world. His knowledgeable and exciting account in *Walden* of what one must do if one is to trade with the Celestial Empire depended on his interest in the trade between New England and China and the East Indies. He wrote in his journal: "When I go to Boston, I go naturally straight through the city down to end of Long Wharf and look off, for I have no cousins in the back alleys. The water and the vessels are novel and interesting. What are our maritime cities but the shops and dwellings of merchants, about a wharf projecting into the sea, where there is a convenient harbor, on which to land the produce of other climes and at which to load the exports of our own? Next in interest to me is the market where the produce of our own country is collected. Boston, New York, Philadelphia, Charleston, New Orleans, and many others are the names of wharves projecting into the sea. They are good places to take in and to discharge a cargo."

"Commerce," he said in *Walden*, "is unexpectedly confident and serene, alert, adventurous, and unwearied," and then he went on to write of the freight train going by Walden Pond on its way from the Long Wharf to Lake Champlain "reminding me of foreign parts, of coral reefs, and Indian oceans, and tropical climes, and the extent of the globe. I feel more like a citizen of the world at the sight of the palmleaf . . . the Manila hemp and cocoanut husks." He enjoyed that great modern improvement of his time the railroad; it was the "pleasantest and wildest road"; there were "no houses or foot-travellers" on it; it was "wild in its accompaniments." And he admired the ease with which it carried great masts to the Navy Yard.

His criticism was not of the improvements themselves, but of men's too great concern for them—a concern, as he made clear in *Walden*, that kept men from examining the quality of their lives: "Men think that it is essential that the *Nation* have commerce, and export ice, and talk through a telegraph, and ride thirty miles an hour, without a doubt, whether *they* do or not; but whether we should live like baboons or like men, is a little uncertain. If we do not . . . forge rails, . . . but go to tinkering upon our *lives* to improve *them*, who will build railroads? But if we stay at home and mind our business, who will want railroads? We do not ride on the railroad; it rides upon us." Emerson put it: "Things are in the saddle." Thoreau admired, but worried.

V

There is no question about what he enjoyed and cherished most, what he thought and wrote about most, what he had no doubts about—that was nature. The banks and reaches of the Concord and Merrimack rivers, the plains and beaches and surfs of Cape Cod, the lakes, rivers, forests, bogs of the Maine woods, and, above all, Concord's "smooth but still varied landscape"—these are the subjects of the great bulk of his writings.

He perceived nature in three ways. One of them is suggested by a statement of Emerson: "The laws of moral nature answer to those of matter as face to face in glass"; that is, he looked at it to discover meanings for men's lives. Sometimes he states the meaning by a metaphor. On surveying the bottom of Walden Pond through the ice, he found that "the line of greatest length intersected the line of greatest breadth exactly at the point of greatest depth." He added: "What I have observed of the pond is no less true in ethics. It is the law of average. Such a rule of the two diameters not only guides us toward the sun in the system and the heart in man, but draw lines through the length and breadth of the aggregate of a man's particular daily behaviors and waves of life into his coves and inlets, and where they intersect will be the height or depth of his character." This mode served for statements of achieved Transcendental intuitions; as in his frequent likening of the periods of the day to the seasons of the year, and the ages of a man's life to both.

But when he wanted to express the unending quest for the experience of the One, of ultimate reality, he wrote in symbols: "We might expect to find in the snow the footprint of a life superior to our own, of which zoology takes no cognizance. Is there no trace of a nobler life than that of an otter or an escaped convict to be looked for in the snow? . . . Why do the vast snow plains give us pleasure, the twilight of the bent and half-buried woods? Is not all there consonant with virtue, justice, purity, courage, magnanimity? Are we not cheered by the sight? And does not all this amount to the track of a higher life than the otter's, a life which has not gone by and left a footprint merely, but is there with its beauty, its music, its perfume, its sweetness, to exhilarate and recreate us? . . . Did this great snow come to reveal the track merely of some timorous hare, or of the Great Hare, whose track no hunter has seen? . . . If one could detect the meaning of the snow would he not be on the trail of some higher life that has been abroad in the night?"

Quite different from these ways of looking at nature was the infinitely detailed recording of the Concord scene. Thoreau wanted to know all his countryside in all its qualities and interrelations. For example, he identified favorite places by natural facts: Arethusa Meadow, Bittern Cliff, Button-bush Pond, Cardinal Shore, Clawshell Bank, Purple Utricularia

Bay, Nut Meadow Brook, Trillium Woods, Yellow-Birch Swamp, Dennis's Lupine Hill. Pages and pages of his journal contain measurements of tree trunks and tree rings, snow depths, and flow of water in the rivers; he made list upon list of the dates of the flowering and fruiting of plants, the migration of birds—he was out in all weathers to gather this information. He noted somewhat wistfully: "It takes many years to find out that Nature repeats herself annually. But how perfectly regular and calculable all her phenomena must appear to a mind that has observed her for a thousand years."

Emerson said quite fairly: "The scale on which his studies proceeded was so large as to require longevity, and we were the less prepared for his sudden disappearance." Thoreau completed only three essays based upon meticulous observation of the regular repetitions of nature: on the succession of forest trees, autumnal tints, and wild apples; they were the work of an untiring and alert observer of the bare, untranscendentalized facts of the natural world—an observer who was aware of a nature that did not *mirror* man but subsumed him. It is particularly fitting that his very last journal entry should record his observation that one could tell the direction of a rain by the disposition of the gravel when the rains were over: "All this is perfectly distinct to an observant eye, and yet could easily pass unnoticed by most."

This third way of perceiving and writing about nature is the one Thoreau most continuously indulged in. He drenched himself in the immediate physical qualities of the natural world that he took in through his senses. He delighted in the fragrances of meadow grasses and the swamp pink; the tastes of huckleberries and wild apples; the infinitely varied songs of birds; the warmth of the November sun in a sheltered spot by the pond; the refreshing coolness of the river's water on a summer day; the ever-changing appearance of the pond, the glowing of the red alder-berry, the flashing air of Quebec.

THOREAU

He was a most sensuous ascetic, like the Jesuit priest and poet, Gerard Manley Hopkins, who saw God's glory in the beauty of the physical world.

Spring

Nothing is so beautiful as Spring—
    When weeds, in wheels, shoot long and lovely and lush;
    Thrush's eggs look little low heavens, and thrush
Through the echoing timber does so rinse and wring
The ear, it strikes like lightnings to hear him sing;
    The glassy peartree leaves and blooms, they brush
    The descending blue; that blue is all in a rush
With richness. . . .

Pied Beauty

Glory be to God for dappled things—
    For skies of couple-colour as a brinded cow;
      For rose-moles all in stipple upon trout that swim;
Fresh-firecoal chestnut-falls; finches' wings;
      Landscape plotted and pieced—fold, fallow, and plough;
      And all trades, their gear and tackle and trim.

Thoreau never lost this delight. He had "the wonderful capacity to appreciate the natural world again and again, with awe, pleasure, wonder, and even ecstasy, however stale these experiences might become to others."

As a result, he loved his place as he thought few others loved theirs. "It is very rare that I hear one express a strong and imperishable attachment to a particular scenery, or to the whole of nature,—I mean such as will control their whole lives and characters. Such seem to have a true home in nature. . . ." He had such a home for his entire life. For his Harvard Class Book he wrote, "If I forget thee, O Concord, let my right hand forget her cunning. . . . To whatever quarter

41

of the world I may wander, I shall deem it good fortune that I hail from Concord North Bridge." Some years later in his journal: "This is my home, my native soil; and I am a New Englander. Of thee, O earth, are my bone and sinew made; to thee, O sun, am I brother. To this dust my body will gladly return as to its origin. Here have I my habitat. I am of thee."

All three ways of looking at nature helped to nourish Thoreau's faith that the future would bring more knowledge and delight. His quest for them was exciting because he did not know exactly what he would find. "How sweet is the perception of a new natural fact! Suggesting what worlds remain to be unveiled. That phenomenon of the andromeda seen against the sun cheers me exceedingly." And, therefore, "the sense of constant expectancy plays on almost every page of his works. . . . He walked the fields like one who was on the alert for some divine apparition. . . ." There were almost infinite possibilities; "How novel and original," Thoreau wrote, "must be each man's view of the universe! For though the world is so old, and so many books have been written, each object appears wholly undescribed to our experience, each field of thought wholly unexplored. The whole world is an America, a *New World.*"

For all his railings against his fellow citizens and the state and the nation, Thoreau's faith and hope in America, the new country, were always dominant. He expressed them in one of his homely metaphors: "I suspect the south pole is the stem end of the globe and that Europe and America are on its rosy cheek, and fortunate are we who live in America, where the bloom is not yet rubbed off." He quoted from one Sir Francis Head: "the heavens of America appear infinitely higher," "the stars are brighter," and added, "These too are encouraging facts, symbolical of the height to which the philosophy and poetry and religion of America's inhabitants may one day soar."

WALT WHITMAN AS AMERICAN

Floyd Stovall

Probably no reader of *Leaves of Grass* would doubt Whitman's Americanism, but whether he was the typical American he claimed to be in the first two editions of his book is a question that requires some study. Hector St. John de Crèvecoeur, who lived in New York and Pennsylvania for a number of years about the time of the Revolution, said, "The American is a new man who acts on new principles; he must therefore entertain new ideas and form new opinions." Of course this new man did not at once become new on arrival in the New World, for he must have brought most of his ideas with him. It was the transplanting of these ideas in a new and fertile soil and their growth in a favorable environment that changed them into something different and seemingly new. The principles, also, that moved men to revolutionary action and that found expression in the Declaration of Independence had their counterparts in the writings of progressive thinkers of eighteenth-century Britain and France.

During the interim between the Declaration and the ratification of the new Constitution, and indeed for several decades afterward, there was much discussion among thoughtful men of an American national character and how it might be recognized. Now that freedom was attained, how could it be made secure and permanent? The Federalists under the leadership of Alexander Hamilton argued that only prosperity and a strong national government could make freedom

43

secure, and indeed prosperity was widespread during the 1790's. When the opposing Democratic-Republican party of Jefferson came into office in 1800 a radical change might have been expected in the direction of the country's development, with more emphasis on the building of an agrarian society and a shift of power from federal to state government. But with the Louisiana Purchase, the Lewis and Clark explorations, and other contributing factors, the West was opened to settlement on a scale undreamed of before; hence the search for wealth continued, especially wealth in the ownership of land, and the federal government, which controlled the new territory, gained more power.

In politics the old Federalist Party gradually evolved into the Whig Party, which was somewhat less conservative, and that eventually into the Republican Party, which was still less conservative. The party of Jefferson, which to begin with was moderately democratic, evolved through the influence of the West toward the equalitarian democracy of Jackson, but was later divided over the question of slavery and its extension into new states carved from the territory of the Louisiana Purchase. In due course the opponents of this extension in both parties merged to form, for a few years, the Free-Soil Party, which was by 1860 absorbed by the new Republican Party. Many historians have said that this period from 1820 to 1860 was the most important in the formation of the American social structure and in the determination of the individual American character. The most notable movement of the time has been described as the rise of the common man. Both the good and the bad qualities of our present society, it has been said, had their roots in this epoch.

Henry Steele Commager, for example, an esteemed historian of American culture, writing from the vantage point of the middle twentieth century, nearly a hundred years after Crèvecoeur, has undertaken in his book *The American Mind* to show that there is a distinctively American way of thought and conduct. Having sloughed off the European traditions of feudalism and nationalism and developed but few local loyalties, Americans, he found, have been rootless and restless, moving from place to place frequently. They have been impatient of small gains, always optimistic, believing in progress but with little sense of history, egotistic, self-reliant, and utilitarian, preferring quantitative to qualitative values, and recklessly destructive of natural resources. Caring little for dogmas or abstract ideas, but fond of organization, they have founded numerous religious denominations among which there are few theological differences. They have, he says, shown considerable talent for politics and respect for law while being themselves often lawless. Although they have recently become confident of the power of education to solve all problems, in the nineteenth century they cared little for higher education and usually preferred the self-made man to the product of colleges. The nineteenth-century American also had great zeal for reform, especially during the decades 1830 to 1860. This was the time when evangelical religions became prevalent. The frontier, precisely because it was the most godless part of the country, became the most fruitful field for the revival preacher, and in the more settled regions, especially in New England, the temperance reformer and the abolitionist were most active.

It is appropriate that Walt Whitman grew from childhood to early manhood during these years and may be said to be a product of the social forces then prevailing. He was born in 1819 on a Long Island farm, attended the public schools of Brooklyn, then a small city, became an apprentice in a local newspaper office, and at the age of sixteen became a journeyman printer in New York City. In 1836 he left the city and for three or four years taught school in communities near his birthplace. He was an eager reader and playgoer, and managed to attend the New York theaters frequently even before he left Brooklyn. While teaching he began to write essays, verses, and stories of the sentimental style then popular, and published some of them in newspapers and magazines. His first and only complete novel was published in 1842 in a single issue of the voluminous newspaper the *New World*, where he was employed as a compositor. It was meant to support the temperance movement, and was called *Franklin Evans; or, The Inebriate*. After he became famous as the author of *Leaves of Grass* he made light of the novel, saying he wrote it in three days with a bottle of liquor on his writing table. Beginning in 1842 he was briefly employed as an editor by a succession of small New York newspapers, but his first important editorial post was with the *Daily Eagle*, an organ of the Democratic Party in Brooklyn. After about two years he lost the position early in 1848, probably because he had become too sympathetic with the Free-Soil principles opposed to the extension of slavery. In February, 1848, he went to New Orleans, where he worked for about three months on a newspaper, the *Crescent*, for which he did routine reporting and wrote feature articles. Returning to Brooklyn, he became active in the Free-Soil organization and for a while edited its newspaper, the *Freeman*.

For three or four years after giving up the *Freeman* Whitman was a free-lance contributor to various periodicals, and for a while the proprietor of a bookstore and a job printing press, but chiefly he was engaged with his father and brothers in housebuilding. Freed from the routine of the editor's desk, he began to read more widely and intensively than before, especially in the British quarterlies—the *Edinburgh Review*, the *North British Review*, the *Westminster Review*, and others—and thereby broadened and enriched his education. The reviews in these quarterlies were original and extensive studies in themselves scarcely less authoritative than the books reviewed, and through them he made acquaintance with much of the learning and some of the best minds of nineteenth-century Europe. He clipped many of these articles so that he could reread and study them at leisure, and on some he made extensive markings and annotations.

At the same time he was cultivating his taste for art and music. He had begun to associate with the young artists of Brooklyn and New York and frequently visited the art galleries and exhibitions of both cities. He came to think of himself as something of an art critic, lectured on art to the members of the Brooklyn Art Union, and then published the lecture in William Cullen Bryant's distinguished paper, the *Evening Post*, on February 1, 1851. It was at this time, perhaps, that he had his first introduction to the sophisticated groups that later called themselves bohemian and made their headquarters at Pfaff's Restaurant on Broadway. These were also the years of his greatest enthusiasm for the Italian opera, where he was thrilled by the magnificent singing of Bettini, Alboni, and Mario, who, he has testified, had great influence on the making of *Leaves of Grass*.

Although Whitman was disillusioned with party politics, he reacted strongly to certain political events that occurred in 1850 and later. On March 2, 1850, Whitman published in the New York *Evening Post* a rhymed poem with the title "Song for Certain Congressmen" in which he stigmatized a number of Northern politicians as "Dough-Faces" because of their willingness to compromise with the Southern faction on slavery. In "Blood-Money," another poem related to the same theme, which he contributed to the *Tribune* on March 22, he implied that certain "betrayers," especially Webster and other supporters of the Fugitive Slave Act of 1850, were the modern equivalents of Judas Iscariot. Also in March he published two other poems in the *Tribune*. One of these, "The House of Friends" (reprinted in *Specimen Days* as "Wounded in the

House of Friends"), was published on June 14, and the other, "Resurgemus," a week later. "The House of Friends" condemns those supposed liberals—he calls them "screamers of Freedom"—who, because of their compromises, are really as bad as the slave owners themselves. "Resurgemus" may be indirectly related to the same theme, but it was more directly a delayed result of his enthusiasm for the European revolutionists of 1848 and his disappointment at their failure. Four years later when, by the authority of the Fugitive Slave Act, Anthony Burns, an escaped slave, was arrested in Boston by a United States marshal and returned to his owner in Virginia, Whitman wrote a very sarcastic poem, later called "A Boston Ballad," ridiculing both the government officials who carried out the action and the people of Boston who allowed it.

Whitman's bitterness was directed less against slavery as established in certain states than against those politicians, both Democratic and Whig, who he feared would, for the sake of compromise, open the doors for the extension of slavery to the new states and territories. His concern was less for the slaves themselves, though that was considerable, than for the white laborers who would be put out of work and deprived of a livelihood by the extension of slavery. It is clear from "The Eighteenth Presidency," which he wrote in 1856 but did not publish, that he was, in his interpretation of the Constitution, a strict constructionist. He was troubled, as have been others, by the apparent difference in the spirit of the Declaration of Independence, which affirmed that all men are born free and equal, and the Constitution, which allowed slavery. He was of course, as an equalitarian, opposed to slavery, but he had come to the conclusion, after 1850, that the problem could not be solved by political means. He had some vague idea that the solution lay in the abolition of political parties as governing bodies, but in "The Eighteenth Presidency" he presented no plan of action except to appeal to the good sense of people, especially working people. He proposed that newspapers print all or parts of his essay, and that rich men put up the necessary money to publish quantities in pamphlet form and distribute them widely. Of course no rich man did, and the essay remained unpublished until the second quarter of the present century.

Whitman's inclusion of "A Boston Ballad" in the first edition of *Leaves of Grass* and the fact that it was composed in June, 1854, justify me in raising again the question that has been debated for more than a century: When did Whitman write the poems that went into this edition? John Townsend Trowbridge, in "Reminiscences of Walt Whitman," published in 1902, asserted that Whitman told him in Boston in 1860 that he began to write out these poems in the summer of 1854, after reading Emerson's essays. He did not say that he first conceived the idea of the poems at this time. He put the matter to Trowbridge this way: "I was simmering, simmering, simmering; Emerson brought me to a boil." I believe this statement is as near the truth as it is possible to come. What it means, as I understand it, is that Whitman had the idea for these poems in his mind before the summer of 1854, albeit perhaps vaguely, and might even have tried his hand at writing a few of them, but that he did not begin to write them out in the form in which they were published until 1854. It is not necessary to assume, from Whitman's remark to Trowbridge, that he had not read Emerson's essays before then; we know in fact that he had read some of them and had also heard Emerson lecture. I take it that Whitman meant that his reading, or rereading, of Emerson's essays in the summer of 1854 was the catalyst that precipitated a new flood of creative energy. The poem "Resurgemus," first published in 1850, also appeared in the 1855 edition in revised form and was later given the title: "Europe, the 72d and 73d Years of These States." The subject matter of this poem is virtually unchanged in the revised version, but the lines are longer and more like the characteristic style of *Leaves of Grass*.

There was ample time between June, 1854, and July, 1855, when *Leaves of Grass* was printed, for Whitman to compose and revise the 2000 to 2500 lines of verse it contained. After his death his literary executors, Dr. Maurice Bucke, Thomas Harned, and Horace Traubel, divided his literary remains equably among themselves, each taking approximately one third of them. Bucke published a large part of his share of the manuscripts in 1899 in a book he called *Notes and Fragments*. Among these scraps are eight or nine hundred lines of what Bucke called "first drafts and rejected lines" of verse. Among these I estimate that nearly one hundred lines are almost identical with lines in the 1855 text—from "Song of Myself" chiefly, together with a few from "The Sleepers," "To Think of Time," and "A Song for Occupations." There are some lines intended for poems not published until 1856, including thirty or forty lines and prose notes for "Song of the Broad-Axe," and a few lines that went into "Salut au Monde!" Several prose passages were incorporated in the 1855 Preface. Another portion of Bucke materials eventually came to Duke University with the Trent Collection, including hundreds of his clippings. Harned's manuscripts, many of them in the form of small homemade notebooks, went to the Library of Congress, where they may still be seen in the original form or in microfilm copies. Emory Holloway published some of them in 1921 in his *Uncollected Poetry and Prose*. In these notebooks appear many notes for poems and perhaps two hundred lines of verse in an advanced stage of completion, later incorporated in "Song of Myself." There are also some lines that appeared first in the 1856 edition in the poem "A Song of the Rolling Earth," and notes for "A Song of Joys." These notebooks certainly predate the first edition, and there is considerable evidence that they were made in 1854. I suspect also that most of the notes for the 1856 poems published in *Notes and Fragments* were written about that time. The manuscripts included in Horace Traubel's share of the remains were kept by him until his death in 1919, since which they have passed through various channels into public libraries, notably the Library of Congress and the New York Public Library.

Throughout Whitman's early years as printer, schoolteacher, editor, politician, and housebuilder, he attempted at intervals to establish himself as a creative writer. Some of the friends of his later years believed, or pretended to believe, that there was some extraordinary change in his mental and spiritual nature between 1848 and 1855, and later biographers have tried to explain the nature and cause of this supposed change. Some have attributed it to a mystical experience, some have supposed a romantic love affair in New Orleans or later, and others have thought they saw reason to suspect the alleged change had something to do with a homosexual attachment that ended in disappointment that found poetic expression in the poems of the Calamus group. His family, however, and friends like the Rome brothers who had known him for years, saw no change in him except what resulted naturally from maturity and education. The fact that he became a dedicated poet is not remarkable, for he had been a poet of sorts since boyhood. It is true that the poetry of *Leaves of Grass* was different from that of his youth and from that of most of his contemporaries, but scholars have pointed many possible sources for his new poetic form, including ancient Hebrew verse, Shakespeare's plays, Macpherson's poems in imitation of Ossian, and certain minor poets of the middle nineteenth century. Throughout the 1840's and early 1850's there was a gradual improvement in his command of English and in his literary style. The language and rhythm of *Leaves of Grass*, as he himself would surely have agreed, have more in common with rhetorical prose than with conventional verse. Critics have been inclined to underrate his early writing and to ignore his sustained ambition. His reading, especially after he left the *Eagle*, was directed primarily to the purpose of preparing himself for a literary career. Once he had become convinced of the rightness of his new style, it was his ambition to become the poet of America and of democracy even as Homer was the poet of classical Greece and Shakespeare of feudal England.

There is a significant prose note in *Notes and Fragments* which Bucke thought was written before 1850, but which more probably dates from 1854. It reads: "Shakespeare and Walter Scott are indeed the limners and recorders—as Homer was one before, and the greatest, perhaps, of any recorder. All belong to the class who depict characters and events and they are masters of the kind. I will be also a master after my own kind, making the poems of emotions, as they pass or stay, the poems of freedom and the exposé of personality—singing in high tones Democracy and the New World of it through These States." This is an accurate statement of Whitman's purpose in *Leaves of Grass*, and was often repeated, in substance, in his Prefaces and in *Democratic Vistas*.

The genius of the United States, Whitman said in his first Preface, is not most or best in its educated classes but in its common people; in their manners, speech, and dress, in their love of freedom and self-esteem, and in their largeness of soul that is in keeping with the largeness of nature. The genius of the American poet is to be commensurate with the people and their land. The poet, not the President, is their representative and proper spokesman. He must be his age transfigured, yet he will show how the present has grown out of the past and how together they form the consistency of the future. In his writing he will be as simple and artless as nature and as uninhibited. Whitman eulogizes the English language, declaring that it is the best tongue in which to express growth, faith, self-esteem, freedom, justice, equality, friendliness, amplitude, prudence, decision, and courage. The last sentence of the Preface turned out to be something of a challenge; "the proof of a poet," he wrote, "is that his country absorbs him as affectionately as he has absorbed it." Apparently he expected the general reading public to like his poems and accept them as characteristically American.

As we know, the public did not, except very tardily. After more than a century, many of the better educated Americans today accept him as one of the best poets of the United States, but the people whom he referred to as "the common people" have never absorbed him, affectionately or otherwise. The reasons are not hard to understand. His style is far from simple, and the language of some of the early poems is often gross if not downright indecent. In "Song of Myself" he represents himself as a true democrat, an equalitarian, a lover and comrade of all men and women, proud but sympathetic, a Christ figure in fact; but he also announces himself as "Walt Whitman . . . one of the roughs," disorderly, fleshly, and sensual. One of the earliest reviewers of the first edition accurately characterized the poems as "a mixture of Yankee transcendentalism and New York rowdyism." If Whitman thought the ferrymen and stagecoach drivers with whom he had associated were typical of the common people, he was mistaken. Even they, however, did not care for the poems, although they liked the poet as a person. Most of the common people then, as now, accepted and tried to practice the conventional manners and morals of the time. What would they have thought of such a line as this: "Divine am I inside and out, and I make holy whatever I touch or am touched from"? Surely they would have thought it both sacrilegious and absurd.

Who, in fact, was this "Walt Whitman," who claimed to have all the vices as well as all the virtues known to man, and who called himself a "kosmos"? He was surely not Walter Whitman, Jr., respected citizen of Brooklyn, sometime editor of local papers, and frequenter of libraries, art galleries, and museums. He was not the actual man who wrote the poems nor a real person at all, but a carefully developed image that had its conceptual beginning in the actual man, but had expanded from that center in all directions. Whitman knew, of course, that this character was not his actual self, but a philosophical projection of that self, to which he added the accretions from years of study and observation, together with a considerable supplement of pure imagination. Walt Whitman was a *persona* created by Walter Whitman to become the embodiment and spokesman of what he assumed to be the democratic doctrine that man, individually and collectively, is both natural and infinitely perfectible. The *persona* Walt Whitman was intended to be a typical American perhaps, but in fact he was generic man in whom all human qualities inhered either actively or potentially. Whitman's assumption was that with the eventual spread of democracy he would become the representative of all men. Democracy would be the religion of a reformed society and the real Walt Whitman would be its poet and evangel.

This image of Walt Whitman continued to be dominant in the poems of the 1856 edition. Although the poet was discouraged at the failure of his first edition to please the common people, he continued to compose new poems, and by the late summer of 1856 his second volume was ready for the printers. It was published by Fowler and Wells in September and contained thirty-two poems, including those originally published in 1855. Some of the new poems were among his best, but the manner in which the book was presented was in poor taste. On the backstrip were these words from Emerson's letter approving the first edition: "I greet you at the beginning of a great career. R. W. Emerson." Within the book, in a section called "Leaves-Droppings," Whitman printed Emerson's entire letter, together with his reply, which Emerson had not yet seen, in which he made ridiculous and false boasts about how well the first edition had sold. In this letter he addressed Emerson as "Master," and claimed to be his disciple, presumptuously implying that Emerson would approve the poems of this second volume, which he had not seen. In spite of this unauthorized use of Emerson's name, the second edition sold no better than the first. He continued to write, but it is obvious from the tone of some of the poems written between September, 1856, and June 1857, that Whitman was discouraged. By the spring of 1857 he was thinking seriously of taking to the lecture platform to preach his democratic religion and to promote his poems, somewhat in the manner Vachel Lindsay would adopt half a century later. The plan for lectures did not materialize, and in May he accepted the position of editor of the Brooklyn *Daily Times*, a non-political paper. This was the year when the country was in the grip of a severe financial panic, when economic conditions were bad, banks failing, and businesses going into bankruptcy. The chances of Whitman's getting out his third edition of *Leaves of Grass* looked slim. But in a surviving note to himself written in June, he warned himself "not to be diverted from the principal object—the main life work," which was, of course, writing poems. On July 20, 1857, he wrote to Mrs. Tyndale, mother of his friend Hector Tyndale, that he had sixty-eight new poems ready for publication, which, together with the thirty-two of the 1856 edition, would make a third edition of one hundred poems. But he had broken with Fowler and Wells, and there was no other publisher available at the time.

The manuscripts of these sixty-eight poems are in the Waller Barrett Collection at the University of Virginia, and in 1955 Fredson Bowers published them along with a detailed textual study that throws considerable light on the probable dates of composition. Early in 1860 Thayer and Eldridge, a publishing firm in Boston, agreed to bring out the third edition. Between July 20, 1857, and March, 1860, when Whitman went to Boston to read proof as the book was being printed, he wrote fifty-four additional poems, making a total of one hundred and fifty-four in the third edition. In this edition the poems were arranged somewhat more logically than they had been in the two earlier editions. The initial poem, a new one, and fairly long, was called "Proto-Leaf," later changed to "Starting from Paumanok." The poem "Walt Whitman," which we know better as "Song of Myself," was relegated to second place. There were five titled groups: "Chants Democratic," containing twenty-one numbered poems; "Leaves of Grass," containing twenty-four; "Enfans d'Adam," later "Children of Adam," containing fifteen; "Calamus," containing forty-five; and "Messenger Leaves," containing thirty-seven miscellaneous short poems. Interspersed between the groups are ten poems of medium length, including three of Whitman's best: "A Word Out of the Sea," later "Out of the Cradle Endlessly Rocking"; "Poem of the Road," later "Song of the Open Road"; and "Crossing Brooklyn Ferry," the last two reprinted from the 1856 edition.

"Proto-Leaf" is explicitly addressed to Americans. After some thirty-five lines introducing himself, Whitman begins his address with the words: "Americanos! Masters! . . . For you a programme of chants." Then he proceeds to catalogue his subjects. There are to be chants to each state from Mexico to Canada, to all contemporary lands, to employments, to sexual organs and acts; to comradeship, which alone, he asserts, must compact the states; and to evil as well as to good. He is to inaugurate a new religion embracing love and democracy; and he will also make the songs of passions, of egotism, of equality, and of the soul, which he declares includes and is the meaning of all. The poems are presented not as spontaneous effusions on unrelated subjects, but as a planned performance designed to produce preconceived effects. Not all the poems can be fitted into the programme, which is much more inclusive than I have just indicated, but most of them can. Among poems previously published "A Song for Occupations," "Salut au Monde," "Song of the Open Road," "To Think of Time," and "Crossing Brooklyn Ferry" illustrate some of the themes mentioned. The new grouping is intended to fit the programme. The "Enfans d'Adam" poems are devoted to sexual topics, "Calamus" to love and comradeship apart from sex, and "Chants Democratic" of course to the theme of democracy, but including such related themes as individualism, nationalism, and religion.

Most of the poems develop their themes directly and so clearly that their meaning is easily understood, but some of the poems, especially the Calamus poems, are symbolic and should not be interpreted literally. Some twentieth-century critics believe they are expressions of homosexual love, not just comradeship, basing their interpretation mostly on a few of the poems. Two of these, No. 4 and No. 9, will suffice to illustrate. In No. 4 the poet represents himself as wandering through the fields and along the side of ponds collecting flowers and plants for lovers, but one plant that grows in or near the ponds he reserves and gives only to those who love as he loves. In poem No. 9 he speaks of being heavy-hearted, discouraged, and distracted because he has learned that the one he cannot content himself without is content without him. The leaves of the calamus plant grow up close together, more or less in the form of a fascicle. Its roots are pink and fragrant. The fascicle is the symbol of comradeship, or friendship, and the fragrance of the roots, which are underground and unseen, is the symbol of love, not sexual, but rather of a spiritual type, what he calls the effusion of the soul. In "Walt Whitman" he says the "perfume" lingering in occupied houses and rooms and even in books on the shelves would intoxicate him if he would let it. Only the atmosphere, symbol of the universal, has no perfume, and hence he bathes in it gladly. These symbols, it seems to me, rather than a literal reading, provide the true meaning of the Calamus poems.

The somber mood of many of the poems of the third edition has sometimes been cited as a probable effect of disappointment in love. But there were other reasons for Whitman to feel discouraged in 1857 and 1858, when many of the poems were written. During the money panic of 1857 Whitman was in financial straits and borrowed $200 from James Parton which he could not repay when his note became due. He was then not only discouraged by the poor reception of his first two editions but also because he was uncertain whether he should be able to finance his third. We know from family letters and other sources that Walt, like his father and like his brother George, was subject to temperamental moods during which he tended to withdraw from others. A number of the poems written between 1857 and 1859 were probably composed during these somber moods, including some of the Calamus poems and such others as "I Sit and Look Out," "A Hand-Mirror," and the poem later called "As I Ebb'd with the Ocean of Life." The close association of love and death, one of the chief characteristics of *Leaves of Grass*, is notable in several of the Calamus poems and in the lovely poem "A Word Out of the Sea," which we know as "Out of the Cradle Endlessly Rocking."

In the themes and in the organization of the third edition we can recognize the influence of phrenology. For ten years or more Whitman had been much interested in that pseudoscience, which sometimes he seems to accept as a genuine science. In July, 1849, Lorenzo Fowler, of the firm of Fowler and Wells, examined Whitman's head and made a phrenological analysis of his character, which has been aptly called his "chart of bumps." Whitman valued this document so highly that he kept it all his life and often referred to it in connection with *Leaves of Grass*. To some extent, I suspect, he conducted his life in accordance with it. The manuscript is now in the Trent Collection at Duke University. Among the characteristics noted by Lorenzo Fowler as prominent in Whitman are amativeness, adhesiveness, self-esteem, caution, combativeness, benevolence, and sublimity; and the entire reading suggests that he was a man of strong and superior qualities. I think it likely that the themes of "Enfans d'Adam," "Calamus," and "Chants Democratic" were programmed to illustrate phrenological categories, especially those which the poet felt to be strong in himself.

Whitman's Children of Adam poems defend sexual love as the condition of life, but they are also concerned with parenthood and the family. The Calamus poems are more intense and passionate than we might expect in poems of comradeship or ordinary friendship, but in the first half of the nineteenth century such sentiment was more common and acceptable than it is now. Both Emerson and Thoreau wrote of friendship in language of emotional intensity and often referred to the feeling of a man for his close friend as love. At times throughout *Leaves of Grass* Whitman appears to become intoxicated with language, especially when writing of democracy, comradeship, egotism, and national pride. Even when his theme is entirely impersonal he tends to exaggerate and to declaim, possibly an imitation, consciously or not, of the manner of Edwin Forrest and other actors he had heard in his youth. Perhaps also it was part of his conception of the *persona* he had created for *Leaves of Grass* and called Walt Whitman.

There is some evidence in the poems of 1860 that Whitman had come to wish to escape from this *persona*, to remove the mask; so in the final poem of the third edition, which became the final poem of all succeeding editions up to and including that of 1881, the speaker, here the *persona*, represents himself as coming from behind the screen of materials, that is as dying. Thenceforth, we are to understand, Whitman will speak in his own person. He has done his work and will depart, leaving the poems, his poetic self, and foretelling other and greater poets to come. It is the *persona* who dies, and the poets to come may suggest that Whitman anticipates the use of other *personae*. In the 1867 edition slight changes were made in the last paragraph, but they do not alter the meaning. In the 1871 edition, however, changes are made which do alter the meaning significantly. In 1860 the third line read, "I feel like one who has done his work—I progress on." The fourth line is new in 1871: "I receive now again of my translations— from my avataras ascending—while others doubtless await me —So long!" In the sixth line, after "Remember my words" he adds, "I may again return." I think the 1860 version of this poem is meant to suggest the removal of the mask previously used, the first *persona*, so that the actual Walt Whitman may speak for himself, and that the revisions made in the 1871 text suggest that the poet thus revealed is an avatar of the essential man. There is also the suggestion that there may be other transformations yet to come.

There was indeed a new poet emerging, and the process was largely completed by Whitman's experiences during the Civil War. Not only the impact of the war itself, but his work among the sick and wounded soldiers in the hospitals of Washington changed him, or at least they changed the image of him we see in the early poems. He acquired a new respect for men as men, not just ideas of men. The courage with which the wounded soldiers endured their sufferings impressed him deeply. During the war he wrote, "I now doubt whether one can get a fair idea of what this war practically is, or what genuine America is, and her character, without some such experience as this I am having." While he was visiting with part of the army at Culpeper, Virginia, in February, 1864, he was awakened one night by the sounds of a detachment of soldiers marching by. Here is part of his record of the experience: "I stood unobserv'd in the darkness and watch'd them long. The mud was very deep . . . along and along they filed by me, with often a laugh, a song, a cheerful word, but never once a murmur. It may have been odd, but I never before so realized the majesty and reality of the American people *en masse*. It fell upon me like a great awe." His confidence in the strength of the American character was lasting. Visiting in New York in 1878 and walking its crowded streets again, he wrote: "To-day, I should say—defiant of cynics and pessimists, and with a full knowledge of all their exceptions—an appreciative and perceptive study of the current humanity of New York gives the directest proof yet of successful Democracy, and of the solution of that paradox, the eligibility of the free and fully developed individual with the paramount aggregate."

One of the effects the War had on Whitman was to deflate his ego. The process had begun before 1860, but it was completed by what he saw of ordinary men making great sacrifices without complaint and performing deeds of heroism without boasting. Another effect was to enlarge his religious horizon and deepen his human sympathies. The poems he wrote during these years and afterward reveal a susceptibility to beauty and an awareness of human goodness that are rare in the early poems. His language became restrained and more formal, sometimes, but not always, at the expense of the vigor and originality of the early work. "When Lilacs Last in the Dooryard Bloom'd," composed in 1865, has both beauty and power, and exhibits Whitman's poetic art at its best. Only a little inferior are "Proud Music of the Storm" and "Passage to India," while many of the short poems of *Drum-Taps* are

Floyd Stovall

equally well executed. The poet of these middle years was, I believe, more nearly the natural and genuine Whitman than the poet of the 1850's. In *Democratic Vistas* and other prose of the postwar years he seemed willing to forego the messianic role of poet-prophet of the new religion of democracy and accept that of the herald of greater poets to come, who shall constitute a priesthood capable of converting the masses to the new religion and transforming our materialistic society into a truly spiritual democracy.

After 1872, though paralysis took its toll, he composed the two major poems, "Prayer of Columbus" and "Song of the Redwood Tree" and a number of well-wrought sea poems, including the group of eight he called "Fancies at Navesink." During these last twenty years of his life, a third *persona* was created, not so much by Whitman himself as by a few adulatory friends who tried to transform his public image into that of a superman, endowed, like the great founders of religions of the past, with cosmic consciousness. The first step in this direction was taken by W. D. O'Connor with the publication in 1866 of his pamphlet *The Good Gray Poet*, a vehement defense of Whitman after he was discharged by the Secretary of the Interior for having published the 1860 *Leaves of Grass*. The work of creating a new *persona* was carried much further by the publication in 1883 of Dr. Maurice Bucke's biography. Bucke was what today we would call a psychiatrist, and was in charge of a Canadian mental hospital. But he was also something of a mystic, and after Whitman's death the author of a book he called *Cosmic Consciousness*. Finally Horace Traubel applied the finishing touches to the image by the publication of his interminable record of Whitman's conversations under the title *With Walt Whitman in Camden*. Whitman was grateful for O'Connor's support, which was needed in the 1860's. He composed portions of Bucke's biography, and he encouraged Traubel to keep his record. At first he may

62

have remonstrated mildly with his friends for their overpraise, but it is possible that eventually he came almost, if not quite, to believe himself the demigod they had created. Many of his old age poems are trivial and probably should never have been allowed to survive. Whitman justified his writing and preserving them on the ground that *Leaves of Grass* was a kind of autobiography, as Bucke said it was. Whether it is autobiographical or not, it provides, together with the poet's prose commentaries, the fullest and most vivid, if not the most accurate, portrait of an American character in our literature.

MELVILLE AND THE AMERICAN
TRAGIC HERO

Leon Howard

Herman Melville is unlike Emerson, Thoreau, and Whitman
in that he was primarily a story-teller rather than a man
with an evangelical message. His stories dealt with American
characters—as well as those of other lands—but not with the
American character. Only in the allegorical *Mardi* does he
appear to be thinking in abstractions. There he satirizes the
passion and greed of American politicians, the "democratic"
principles which enable any citizen to pull the nose of his
President and require the President to put up with such rude
familiarity, and, above all, the American conviction that freedom is the product of republican institutions instead of ex-
panding frontiers. It is difficult to know how seriously we
should take Melville's sardonic attitude toward the excessive
egalitarianism and chauvinism of his day, but we can be sure
of his belief that a common American could be as heroic as
one of the kings or princes of Greek or Shakespearean drama.

Such a heroic figure, of course, is Captain Ahab of *Moby-
Dick*—that "grand, ungodly, god-like man" who has fasci-
nated so many readers in so many ways and has created in me
a life-long curiosity about the way he came into being and the
way he has affected readers of at least two later generations.
The results of my effort to satisfy this curiosity are what I
want to present here. They involve the story of the creation of

65

a novel (a story which I am afraid I have already told too often), a newer story of a character's evolution within the book, and the consideration of a unique artistic accomplishment which has characteristics peculiarly able to affect readers today.

Moby-Dick was the sixth of Melville's romances. The first five had been written in the five years following his discharge from the United States Navy in the autumn of 1844, the last two having been composed rapidly and under great pressure during the spring and summer of 1849 while Melville was cooped up with his large family of dependents and an epidemic of blue cholera raged around them in the sweltering heat of New York City. He needed a vacation and hoped to earn one by taking the proof-sheets of his latest book, *White-Jacket* to London and making a better bargain for it, in person, than he had recently got for *Redburn*. Despite the bad weather at the beginning of the voyage, Melville soon had his sea legs back and enjoyed the run of the ship which the captain allowed him. At the age of thirty he was still boyish enough to astonish the other passengers by scampering up the rigging, and he had been secluded long enough to be excited by the opportunity for talking with the passengers—especially two young transcendentalists whose acquaintance he continued to cultivate after the voyage was over. He was successful in his negotiation for *White-Jacket* and probably talked with his publisher about plans for his next book. He had been taking notes for the novel which much later became *Israel Potter*, but at some time during the trip he changed his plans—whether because of a "sea feeling" that came over him or because of his publisher's advice we do not know—and decided to write a book about whaling and some of the romantic legends associated with it.

It is reasonable to assume, therefore, that Melville planned his new book in January, 1850, as he paced the cold deck of the packet ship *Independence* on his voyage home. In any event he went promptly to work after landing in New York on the first of February, and by May 1 he was able to write Richard Henry Dana, Jr., that he was "half way in the work." On June 27 he promised his English publisher for "the latter part of the coming autumn" a book which he described as "a romance of adventure founded upon certain wild legends in the Southern Sperm Whale Fisheries" and illustrated by his "own personal experience, of two years and more, as a harpooneer." Melville was always optimistic, especially when writing to his publisher, about the date for completing a book, but on this occasion he was sufficiently sure of himself to plan a vacation in the western part of Massachusetts for the latter part of July and early August. There, at Pittsfield in the Berkshires, Evert Duyckinck, editor of the New York *Literary World*, saw the unfinished manuscript and wrote his brother George on August 7, 1850, that "Melville has a new book mostly done—a romantic, fanciful and literal and most enjoyable presentment of the Whale Fishery—something quite new."

Precisely what part or parts of the book remained undone we do not know. With the possible exception of the two quickly written recent books, Melville had never written a complete book seriatim—that is, page by page or chapter by chapter as it appeared in its printed form—and he certainly planned to make insertions in his new one because he was nearly halfway through it before he began completing his collection of reference books on whaling. The most frequently used of these arrived on the very eve of his vacation, and his use of it and of another obviously influential book (Carlyle's *Sartor Resartus*, which he borrowed at about the same time) has enabled scholars to identify much of the material he necessarily added after the work was "mostly done." Some of this consisted of whole chapters or groups of chapters, some might

have been sentences or paragraphs, and some represented revisions of single words and phrases. Melville, in fact, found
it hard to let go his manuscript. He kept adding footnotes after
the book had been partly printed and it had become too ex-
pensive to work new observations into the text; and as late
as June 14, 1851, more than ten months after Duyckinck's
visit, he wrote Hawthorne that he was adding "shanties of
chapters and essays" in order to hold it together.

Why should he have worked for more than ten additional
months on a book which he had considered "mostly done" in
about five? The answer surely lies in the new direction his
work took during these months when he quit referring to it
as a story of the "whale fisheries" and began to call it his story
of "the whale." The legend of the great white whale of the
Pacific—Mocha Dick, as J. N. Reynolds had called him—was
evidently much more important in the second version of the
novel than it had been in the first. There is considerable
evidence to support the hypothesis that the *Town-Ho*'s story
(which appears as Chapter 54 in the published book) approxi-
mates the story of the *Pequod* as Melville originally planned
it and foreshadowed it in the opening chapters of his finished
narrative. But as the whale increased in importance the conventional human conflicts between captain and crew, mates
and men, became relatively insignificant. The original plan
had to change.

The reason for the change may be found in a new inspira-
tion and new ambition which came to Melville during his
vacation in the Berkshires, and it may be traced to the events
of a single day. Melville had invited two of his New York
literary friends, Evert Duyckinck and Cornelius Mathews, to
spend a week with him on his cousin's farm; and a neighbor,
David Dudley Field, undertook to entertain them and other
literary people in the Berkshires. The entertainment was to
consist of a morning climb to the top of nearby Monument

Mountain, and an elaborate dinner at Field's afterwards. As the group approached the top of the mountain a sudden thunder storm forced them to take refuge in a narrow cave, and there Oliver Wendell Holmes unlatched the black medical bag he had been carrying and produced champagne and a silver mug. It could hardly have been enough to refresh the whole party of ten, and Melville, Holmes, and Nathaniel Hawthorne apparently had more than their share. In any event, when they reached the top these three began to behave in an odd way. Holmes peered over the sheer cliff on one side of the summit (which was the local lover's leap) and described, in medical terms, the symptoms of vertigo. Hawthorne gazed mildly around looking for "the great carbuncle" about which he had written a story more than a dozen years before. Melville ran out on a projecting rock and began hauling on imaginary rigging.

It was a gay occasion until Cornelius Mathews, a pompous little man in glasses, spoiled it by producing a copy of William Cullen Bryant's poems and insisting upon reading a long and dull poem about two Indian lovers who had leaped over the cliff which Holmes and Melville had been treating so irreverently. This led to an unrecorded response by Holmes (who was another little man, but as sprightly as Mathews was dull) and eventually to a literary quarrel between the New Yorkers and the New Englanders which lasted all the way down the mountain and throughout the long and "well liquified" dinner that followed.

The basic difference of opinion between the two groups was over a major critical theory of the time—the influence of climate on genius. The New Yorkers, as befitting the residents of a city which was soon to produce Walt Whitman, believed that America would produce a literature which would be as majestic as its mountains and as mighty as it rivers. The New Englanders, especially Holmes, were skeptical—although Holmes did admit, in a Phi Beta Kappa poem delivered ten days later, that New York's critics were as foggy as its atmosphere. The debate finally settled upon the question whether America ever would or could produce another Shakespeare, and the only agreement reached was that if a nineteenth-century Shakespeare appeared anywhere he would use the most popular literary form of the time and appear as a novelist rather than as a dramatist.

The day's events had a profound effect upon Melville. They evidently caused him to think more about literature—its form and its substance—than he had thought while composing his autobiographical romances and the "chartless voyage" of his allegorical *Mardi.* He had developed an inclination toward Elizabethan writers during the past two years when he was living in New York City, and he now began to think seriously about the possibility of an American Shakespeare. He was not as chauvinistic as his New York friends, but he was less of an anglophile than the New Englanders. He was excited by the lively exchange of ideas and opinions and was even more excited by his first meeting with Nathaniel Hawthorne.

Hawthorne was fifteen years older than Melville and was living in the nearby town of Lennox. Melville had a superficial acquaintance with his stories but had not read them carefully, and his Aunt Mary had given him, at the beginning of his visit, a copy of *Mosses from an Old Manse,* which he had not yet read. After meeting the man Melville turned to the book and read it under the influence of the previous day's excitement. In it he found a man who came close to being the American Shakespeare about whom his friends had been speculating: "Shakespeare has been approached," he announced in a review of the *Mosses* for the *Literary World*: "Not a very great deal more, and Nathaniel were verily William." In "the great Art of Telling the Truth," he believed, Hawthorne had actually exceeded Shakespeare. Melville's interest in the "dark conceit" or hidden allegory of *The Faerie Queene* had convinced him that "all men wore muzzles in the Elizabethan day" and therefore that Shakespeare could reveal the "blackness" of "Truth" in his greatest tragedies only "covertly and by snatches." The modern Hawthorne, however, could express himself more directly in the "appalling" moral of "Earth's Holocaust" (which taught that the evils of the world were derived from "the all-engendering heart of man") and in the "profound" implications of "Young Goodman Brown," who saw evil beneath all good appearance but could not be sure whether it was really there or in his own mind.

This review of a book four years old (which was printed anonymously as by "a Virginian" who professed never to have seen Hawthorne) showed that Melville had begun speculating immediately after Field's party about the appearance of a Shakespeare in modern American dress whose tragic force would be derived from an intuition of the "blackness" beyond everyday appearances and its appeal to "that Calvinistic sense of Innate Depravity and Original Sin, from whose visitations, in some shape or other, no deeply thinking mind is always and wholly free." This was different from the transcendental optimism of Emerson and Thoreau and the more rational optimism of Whitman, and Melville was not at all sure whether Hawthorne was using this "mystical blackness" as a literary device or whether "there really lurks in him, perhaps unknown to himself, a touch of Puritanic gloom." Nor did he, despite all his talk about truth-telling and "the blackness of darkness beyond," commit himself, in all moods, to this attitude. But this is the point from which his new artistic meditations took their departure.

At one time I believed that Melville's plan for a Shakespearean tragedy in the form of a modern American novel was conceived at once and said, rather melodramatically, that the events of this first week in August "triggered his explosion into greatness." Now I have learned better. It would be more accurate to say that they lit a slow fuse which smoldered and sputtered through the fall and well into the winter before the charge was really set off.

Melville had little time for writing during the rest of the summer and could not have met his original deadline for completing his book even if his plans had remained unchanged. He found an opportunity to buy the farm next to his cousin's and decided to do so and move his large family of mother and four sisters, wife and child to the country. Moving and getting settled took up most of his time and energy. On Sunday, October 6, he wrote Duyckinck that he had hardly been able to "find time or *table* to write you this long while." Yet he had spent the day, as he put it, "*Jacquesizing* in the woods"; and the allusion to *As You Like It* suggests that he was not only thinking long and seriously about something beyond the ordinary chores of setting his farm to rights and helping his women move furniture but thinking in Shakespearean terms. He expected it to be another month, though, before he would be through with his work in the open air.

Yet a man of his habits would have found some time for reading, and it was probably during this period that he read and marked his recently acquired and still extant copy of Thomas Beale's *Natural History of the Sperm Whale* which provided him with so much usable material for his revised book. He also had Carlyle's *Sartor Resartus* at hand and read that, if we can judge by the way and frequency with which he used it, with interest and delight. He had more time for browsing in Shakespeare than Jacquesizing in the woods, for the set in "glorious great type" which he had bought a year and a half before provided him with three of the few volumes he could read by candlelight.

When cold weather set in there was nothing to keep him

from a regular daily stint of writing which began after the morning chores and lasted for five or six continuous hours. He would naturally have been concerned with the technical information about whaling that he had planned to introduce into his earlier mansucript, and he undoubtedly increased the amount of this, far beyond his original plans, after he learned from Carlyle the trick of treating dull stuff with sardonic whimsicality. By December 13 he was working with enthusiasm. "Can you send me about fifty fast-writing youths, with an easy style and not averse to polishing their labors?" he asked Duyckinck on that day. He had "planned about that number of future works" but could not find time to think about them separately. At the moment he was probably being carried away by "The Honor and Glory of Whaling" (his title for Chapter 82) because three days later (as he tells us in a parenthesis) he was beginning Chapter 85, "The Fountain." He had discovered "a sort of sea-feeling" in the snow-covered countryside, he told Duyckinck, and was responding to it not only by writing energetically but by scampering through his intellectual rigging.

So far we have been on fairly firm ground—insomuch as it possible to follow a writer's creative activity by inferences based upon circumstantial evidence. It would be a reasonable guess that about two-thirds of the descriptive and discursive chapters which form the central section of *Moby-Dick*—those between the time the *Pequod* gets underway and Ahab gets a new leg and the narrative a new start—were written during the fall and early winter when Melville's mind was going off in various directions; and this would also be the most likely time for him to have written the chapters in dramatic form which suggest that Melville was trying to be Shakespearean without knowing how. But none of this evidence provides any indication of Captain Ahab's place in the narrative.

Ahab, in one characterization or another, was certainly in

the story from its very beginning. A ship must have a captain, and in the course of a long voyage, such as that of a whaler, everything relating to the morale of the ship eventually focuses upon him. His authority at sea is absolute, and he is and must be at times a tyrant. Melville had sailed under at least two captains whose tyranny he considered unreasonable and had found another in the "Captain A————" of John Ross Browne's *Etchings of a Whaling Cruise*, which had set a course for the *Pequod* and provided the staging for Ahab's first appearance on the quarter deck. Such a realistic character could easily have been transformed into a more romantic wanderer of his own dark mind with a Byronic clump and a strange power over weird oriental followers. But such a transformation would not have given him Shakespearean stature or made him the profoundly tragic hero he became. A clue to the evolution of Captain Ahab must be sought in some of the more specific influences which affected his creation.

There were two of these. One was Carlyle's *Sartor Resartus*, which, as we know, deeply affected Melville in the latter part of 1850, just as it had already affected the Emerson of *Nature* and the Thoreau of Walden Pond. The other was Samuel Taylor Coleridge's *Notes and Lectures upon Shakespeare*, especially the lecture on *Hamlet*, which Melville read and meditated on at some still undetermined time. Since the Coleridge influence was basic to the dramatization of Ahab, we should first consider what Coleridge had to say about how Shakespeare went about imagining a tragic hero: "one of Shakespeare's modes of creating characters," he said, "is to conceive any one intellectual or moral faculty in morbid excess, and then to place himself . . . thus mutilated or diseased, under given circumstances." Melville echoed this language in his first reference (in Chapter 16) to Ahab as "a mighty pageant character, formed for noble tragedies": "Nor will it at all detract from him, dramatically regarded, if either by birth or circumstances, he have what seems a half wilful, over-ruling morbidness at the bottom of his nature. For all men tragically great [he added] are made so by a certain morbidness. Be sure of this, O young ambition, all mortal greatness is but disease." He echoed Coleridge again in Chapter 41 when he had Ishmael explain the Captain's behavior by saying that ever since his almost fatal encounter with Moby-Dick "Ahab had cherished a wild vindictiveness against the whale, all the more fell for that in his frantic morbidness he at last came to identify with him, not only all his bodily woes, but all his intellectual and spiritual exasperations." "All that most maddens and torments; all that stirs up the lees of things, all truth with malice in it; all that cracks the sinews and cakes the brain; all the subtle demonisms of life and thought; all evil, to crazy Ahab, were visibly personified, and made practically assailable in Moby-Dick" because Ahab had deliriously transferred their idea to "the abhorred white whale" and "pitted himself, all mutilated, against it."

However near the beginning these passages were placed in the final narrative, they could hardly have been written before Melville read Coleridge's essay. When he did so, however, is a moot question. The earliest date the *Lectures on Shakespeare* are known to have been available to him is November 27, 1852, when his father-in-law charged the book out from the Boston Athenaeum while Melville was in Boston and thinking about writing the story of Agatha Robinson. It is possible, though, that he turned to Coleridge on that occasion because he had used him earlier when he had been troubled by a similar problem in characterization. If so, the most probable time would have been around Christmas, 1850, when he joined his wife and baby in Boston, just after completing the cluster of chapters including "The Fountain," and could have paid a personal, though unrecorded, visit with Judge Shaw to the Athenaeum library. The nearest guess we can make, then, about the beginning of Ahab's transformation into a Shakespearean tragic hero is that it occurred sometime after the first of the year when Melville was about halfway through the revision of his novel.

Melville may have got some suggestion for Ahab's intellectual mutilation and morbid disease from the one attributed to Hamlet, who, as Coleridge explained him, "looks upon external things as hieroglyphics" and whose mind, from its "everlasting broodings," had become "unseated from its healthy relations" and "constantly occupied with the world within" gave "substance to shadows." But Ahab is no Hamlet who can't decide whether to suffer outrageous fortune or take arms against a sea of troubles. Melville found a more modern and timely prototype for him in the hero of *Sartor Resartus*, who, when he felt like an outcast in a world claimed by the devil, stood up in his "native God-created majesty" and with his "whole Me" exclaimed: "*I* am not thine, but Free, and forever hate thee!" It was at this time, when he said "No" thunder to the forces of evil which claimed his spirit, that Carlyle's hero said he "began to be a Man."

Carlyle's professor had taught that "All visible things are emblems" and that "Matter exists only spiritually, and to represent some Idea, and *body* it forth." Melville's captain used the same conception of an emblematic universe in order to explain himself to Starbuck: "All visible objects, man, are but as pasteboard masks." In the White Whale which had mutilated him on a previous voyage he saw "outrageous strength, with an inscrutable malice sinewing it." And this was what he was defying: "That inscrutable thing is chiefly what I hate; and be the white whale agent, or be the white whale principal, I will wreak that hate upon him." Later in one of the last and most dramatic chapters of the book Ahab was to defy the lightning and everything it symbolized, thereby achieving the "Baphometic Fire-baptism" which Carlyle's hero symbolically received when he defied the "Everlasting No." Captain Ahab has a distinct resemblance to Professor Teufelsdröckh at this stage in the latter's development. The chief difference is that Ahab remained in this stage instead of passing through it and into a stage of more optimistic transcendental faith.

The significance of these literary influences is that they reveal Melville's deliberate efforts to transform the captain of the *Pequod* from the conventional (though perhaps romanticized) tyrant over his crew into a dramatic hero who could be engaged in some larger struggle and with whom the author and reader could more readily identify themselves. The method, derived from Coleridge, was that of creating an imperfect character whom he could admire while being aware of his imperfection. The imperfection, suggested by Carlyle, was an intuitive perception of the universe (comparable to that of a person in the first stage of a religious conversion) which would bring out the heroic qualities of a great man but drive a lesser one to despair. We do not know of Melville, any more than he knew of Hawthorne, whether his use of this "mystical blackness" was a literary device or whether he himself had a lurking touch of "Puritanic gloom." We do know, however, that Ahab's vision of the "blackness beyond" the visible reality of the White Whale was Ahab's tragic flaw.

This tragic flaw was one that anybody might possess, but in all other respects Ahab is a thoroughly American hero. Although he bears the name of a king, he is introduced as an uncommon common man—a "fighting Quaker" from Nantucket, one of "the most sanguinary of all sailors and whalehunters" who speaks in the "stately dramatic" idiom of his sect and has not only experienced violent action but the strange thoughts that come during "long night-watches in remotest waters." Such a man "of greatly superior natural force" with "a bold and nervous natural language," he said, was "one in a whole nation's census—a mighty pageant creature formed for noble tragedies." In the concluding paragraphs of Chapter 26 (certainly written after he had soaked himself in Carlyle) he considers the dignity of tragedy and the high place of the hero: "this august dignity I treat of, is not the dignity of kings and robes . . . but that democratic dignity which, on all hands, radiates without end from God" whose omnipresence is "our divine equality." And in his effort to "ascribe high qualities, though dark" to "meanest mariners, and renegades and castaways," and "weave round them tragic graces," he invoked (for protection against "all mortal critics") the "Spirit of Equality" and the "great democratic God": "Thou who didst pick up Andrew Jackson from the pebbles; who didst hurl him upon a warhorse; who didst thunder him higher than a throne! Thou, who in all Thy mighty earthly marchings, ever cullst Thy selected champions from the kingly commons; bear me out in it, O God!"

Whether the drama of Captain Ahab would have been improved by the discipline of the stage (as Melville's friend Duyckinck said it would in his shocked review of the greatly expanded book) I do not know. But I am sure that it would not have made the impression it has made upon the twentieth-century consciousness if it had appeared in any other context than that of the unconventional novel form which contains it. For Melville, in attempting to write a Shakespearean novel, created something unique: *Moby-Dick* is the only example of eighteenth or nineteenth century fiction which contains two completely different characters with whom the author could identify himself at will. One of these, of course, is Ishmael the narrator, who is not unlike the *persona* Melville adopted and used to express his opinions in all his autobiographical romances. The other is Ahab, a "sovereign nature" with whom Melville had so closely identified himself by the middle of April, 1851, that he could refer to him indiscriminately as "he" or "me." Such a man, Melville wrote Hawthorne, "may

78

perish; but so long as he exists he insists upon treating with all Powers on an equal basis. If any of those other Powers choose to withold certain secrets, let them; that does not impair my sovereignty in myself; that does not make me tributary."

Neither of these characters represented that mysterious entity (if there is any such thing) which some people would like to call "the real Melville." But with the two of them Melville achieved an extraordinary range of emotional and intellectual expression. He could put on the disguise of Ahab and "rant" in what he considered true Elizabethan style. Or, in the *persona* of Ishmael, he could relax into the subjectivity and self-consciousness of a nineteenth-century story-teller, being reflective, informative, and amusing as the spirit moved him, but with an underlying intensity characteristic of the new apprenticeship novels of Goethe and Carlyle. His realistic presentment of the whale fisheries had not only become a romance of epic proportions but a tragic drama and something of a *Bildungsroman* as well. It was an artistic form which enabled an unusually complex writer to give full range to his emotions, his mind, and his rhetoric. No other novelist has achieved it.

The achievement was not appreciated in Melville's own day. Though praised by some critics for one reason or another, *Moby-Dick* was condemned by most; and during Melville's lifetime it sold less well than *Typee, Omoo, White-Jacket,* and *Redburn,* and only slightly better than *Mardi.* It was first recognized as one of the world's great novels more than two generations after its publication and a generation after Melville's death—when a new century had intensified the contradictions, ambiguities, and tensions which Melville's contemporaries were not prepared to recognize in his book. Even today critics and readers will argue about the "meaning" of *Moby-Dick* under an assumption that the novel must be unified by some intellectual conviction rather than by the artist's sensitivity to an intellectual climate which was in the process of developing.

The somewhat schizophrenic climate of our century is one which Melville anticipated in two ways through his involvement in such different characters as Ahab and Ishmael. Melville's ability to express some of his most profound thoughts and daring emotions in the person of Ahab and then, in the person of Ishmael, stand aside and call himself a crazy monomaniac is an artistic anticipation of the great question which many of us sometimes have to face: If I am hell-bent on doing something, should I go at it or go to a psychiatrist? Or, in another form, should a man of great natural force and determination, driven by some deep conviction, be admired and followed or cut down to size? We all have our obsessions. There is a White Whale on or just below the horizon of everyman, and when we get together in some highly emotionalized group it is usually in pursuit of a monstrous one. Should we chase it, wholeheartedly, with Ahab? Or take thought, like Hamlet?

Another way in which Melville anticipated the modern dilemma is to be seen in the contrasting mental qualities he attributes to Ahab and Ishmael, the two characters with whom he identifies himself. Ahab thinks in symbols. Carlyle and Emerson moralized about the symbolic nature of the universe, but they did not think symbolically. Ahab did. The abstraction of the great White Whale was more real to him than the monster himself. Melville could never have prophesied that Ahab's short cut to reality would be used to split the atom and put it together again in an explosion which would jeopardize civilization, or that it would be used to put a man on the moon. Nor could he have foreseen the extent to which symbols of race, religion, and rival economic systems would become inscrutable monsters in the minds of many men. Although we are closer to Ishmael than to Ahab in our everyday thoughts, we think in symbols far more than men of the nine-

teenth century did and have broken down the distinction between an objective reality and one which is the creation of our
own minds—not because we are mad but because experimental
scientists have shown that the mathematician's symbols may
have a practical and manageable reality. But outside the labo-
ratory, in the more complicated world of human beings, we
have no way of determining whether our chosen symbols
represent intuitive short cuts to the truth or neurotic refusals
to face the facts of an environment too complex to be understood by observation and reflection. We live in Ahab's world
far more than Melville and his contemporaries did, but we
continue to share Ishmael's skepticism about it.

Even Ahab was not altogether sure of himself. In his first
statement of defiance he confessed that he sometimes thought
there was "naught beyond" the symbol that haunted him. In
his last reference to the "inscrutable" thing which drove him
(just before the beginning of the final chase) he thought that
it might possibly be something within him. "Is Ahab, Ahab?"
he asked. "Is it I, God, or who, that lifts this arm?" Yet his
determination was unshakable. It overrode the good sense of
his first mate and inspired his motley crew, and even the
skeptic Ishmael, his analyst, became his boatsteerer on the last
fatal day of the chase. Melville admired him, as he professed
to admire all men who were willing to "cross the frontiers into
Eternity with nothing but . . . the Ego." The fact that Ahab
was willing to do so—the fact that he would declare himself
"a sovereign nature . . . amid the powers of heaven, hell, and
earth" and treat with them upon an equal basis—made him a
hero. The fact that he could rise to such heights solely on the
strength of his ego—that self-reliance which Emerson praised,
Thoreau practiced, and Whitman symbolized—made him, in
Melville's eyes, an American hero. But he never discovered
the secret that lay behind the emblematic appearance of the
physical universe or learned whether there was, in fact, any

secret at all. He preserved his sovereignty in himself but in doing so destroyed himself, the *Pequod*, and all its crew. Melville raises more questions than he answers in *Moby-Dick*, and one of them seems to be whether anybody can be a hero at all, in America, without being a tragic one.